THE NEW WORLD

THE NEW WORLD

◆◆◆◆◆◆◆◆◆◆◆◆◆◆◆◆◆◆◆◆

AN EPIC POEM

by

Frederick Turner

PRINCETON UNIVERSITY PRESS

PRINCETON, NEW JERSEY

PRINCETON SERIES OF CONTEMPORARY POETS
(For other books in the series, see page 183)

◆

Copyright © 1985 by Princeton University Press

Published by Princeton University Press, 41 William Street,
Princeton, New Jersey 08540
In the United Kingdom: Princeton University Press, Guildford, Surrey

Library of Congress Cataloging in Publication Data will be
found on the last printed page of this book

ISBN 0-691-06641-8
ISBN 0-691-01420-5 (pbk.)

Publication of this book has been aided by a grant from
The Paul Mellon Fund of Princeton University Press

This book has been composed in Linotron Galliard

Clothbound editions of Princeton University Press books are printed
on acid-free paper, and binding materials are chosen for strength and
durability. Paperbacks, although satisfactory for personal collections,
are not usually suitable for library rebinding

Printed in the United States of America by
Princeton University Press
Princeton, New Jersey

The author acknowledges with gratitude the assistance of Carl
Djerassi and the trustees of the Djerassi Foundation

Contents

The New World

AN INTRODUCTORY NOTE ON ITS PURPOSES, GENRE, ARGUMENT, AND SETTING

The fundamental purpose of *The New World* is to demonstrate that a viable human future, a possible history, however imperfect, does lie beyond our present horizon of apparent cultural exhaustion and nuclear holocaust. Art has the world-saving function of imaginatively construct-ing other futures that do not involve the Götterdämmerung of mass su-icide; because if there is no other imaginative future, we will surely in-deed *choose* destruction, being as we are creatures of imagination.

To think of a poem doing something like this is to take a step be-yond the short free verse existentialist imagist lyric poem which has dominated the modernist period in literature. That period is, perhaps, coming to an end—partly because its ideas, bold and splendid as they were, could not protect us from our threat to destroy ourselves. *The New World* is an epic poem, and is intended to serve as an opening to a post-modern creative era.

There are many things that poetry can do that cannot be done by any other literary form. The novel cannot do them; it does not have fully at its disposal the capacities of poetic meter, image, symbol, and allusion; the poetic freedoms offered by figurative language and compression; the mysterious affective forces of dream and vision; and the poetic power to change the very ground rules of the game. If the novel is like natu-ralistic stage drama, and if the lyric poem is like instrumental art music, the epic poem is like opera, a unique form of its own. It may be the most potent instrument for creating those alternate or subjective worlds which we now need to substitute for the holocaust in our future.

The New World attempts not to create a utopia but to suggest the surprises of history, its mysterious potential, and its real, if unexpected response to our own choices, decisions, dreams, and desires. It depicts a world, like ours, of good and evil; but of goods and evils wildly differ-ent from our own, and thus perhaps imaginatively liberating. And it also shows within those differences the persistence of the miracle of hu-man value.

The meter of *The New World* is based on an enjambed long line di-vided by a caesura, as is appropriate for epic poetry (for good neurolog-ical/ethological reasons, as the author argues in an essay "The Neural Lyre" in *Poetry*, August 1983). It is related to the meters of *Sir Gawaine and the Green Knight, El Cid,* the *Iliad,* and the *Aeneid.* Each line contains five heavy stresses and up to ten or so light stresses. The classic iambic pentameter of Shakespeare and Milton is a "special case" of this meter, and indeed much of the quoted narration of the character James George Quincy is in pentameter.

Readers familiar with the style of the lyric poem—its unity of tone, the ambiguity, intensity, and difficulty of its language, and its avoidance of discursive, narrative, and conversational diction—may find the epic style of *The New World* rather peculiar at first. The epic uses not only the "middle style" usual for the lyric, but also the "low style" of the comic and "high style" of the heroic, as well as the "plain style" of direct statement. Much of the pleasure of epic lies in its transitions from style to style, the variations in its intensity, the contrasts between passages of lyric density and passages of narrative simplicity or philosophical complexity. Only by using this broad range of diction can the epic accomplish its purpose of presenting a whole world in all its rich differences.

The poem is set four hundred years in the future, in a version of the classical "epic interval" of two hundred to one thousand years between the subject and the composition of the poem. The "epic interval" of *The New World* is unique in that it projects the action into a subjunctive or possible future, not into the past. American culture is celebrated in *The New World* as *Beowulf* celebrates the Nordic, Virgil the Roman, and Homer the Greek cultures. As Aeneas' journey to Italy gives meaning to the Rome of Virgil and Augustus, so *The New World*'s future makes sense of our present. *The New World* represents a swing of the epic poem away from the self-regard or self-concern of Wordsworth's *Prelude* and Eliot's shattered mini-epic *The Waste Land,* toward a new kind of outward glance at the world.

The plot of the poem is related to several great stories: the Odysseus story, of a man who must struggle to return home and claim his family from his enemies; the Icelandic story of Burnt Njal, a tragic family feud; the story of Parsifal, in which it is not the hero's prowess but his questions that enable him to find the Grail; the story of Snow White, the princess who is put to sleep by a witch; the story of Arjuna and Krishna, in which a hero weary of war is able to reconcile his duty with his knowledge; the story of Queen Elizabeth I, who gave up her personal life for her people; the story of the American Civil War; and innumerable American Frontier stories of testing, revenge, justice, and sacrifice. It is also a romance, a love story that deals with the relationship between desire, psychic damage, public duty, pride, and love.

The theme of *The New World*, inasmuch as it can be briefly summarized, is the discovery of a third mode of knowledge, belief, and commitment that transcends the contemporary dilemma of fanatical blind faith and affectless hedonistic relativism. This third mode might be called the performative mode, since it performs its own truth and is self-fulfilling, makes possible joyful action and meaningful values without blinking at the brevity and contingency of life. It does not dismiss the human desire for closure, certainty, and goals, as certain modern moral philosophers have done, nor does it permit that desire to stunt and narrow existence; rather, it uses that desire as the energy required for sacrifice, and it asserts that only sacrifice can bring about a life that is rich, concrete, and esthetically satisfying.

◆

The story opens in the year 2376 A.D. The world's fossil and nuclear fuels have been spent, its metallic ores exhausted, and much of its population either departed for the stars or slaughtered in the great twentieth- and twenty-first-century pogroms against the middle class. But high civilizations, based on a technology of solar and wind power, glass and resin chemistry, microprocessors and bioengineering, still flower on the earth. War is waged by mounted knights in resinite armor, with lasers and swords. The ancient institution of the nation state, obeying the same historical laws that brought it into existence, has collapsed, and the human race has discovered new forms of political organization: the Riots—violent matriarchies based in the ancient cities, whose members have no incest prohibitions and no money, are addicted to the psychedelic joyjuice, and have almost lost the power of human language; the Burbs—populations descended from the old middle class, whom the Riots hold hostage and use as slaves to produce their food, luxuries, and joyjuice; the Mad Counties—religious theocracies, dominated, in North America, by fanatical fundamentalists; and the Free Counties—independent Jeffersonian aristocratic democracies, where art, science, and the graces of human life are cultivated to their highest, as in classical Athens, Renaissance Florence, and Heian Japan. The Free Counties have developed a new religion of their own, combining science, Christianity, Judaism, Buddhism, and the other major religions. Under the influence of the great oriental cultures, the implicit divisions of American society have emerged explicitly in a caste system, comprising the Kshatriyas or warrior-guardians, the

Brahmins or priests, the Vaisyas or merchants, and the Shudras or farmers.

A league of Mad Counties in the area known as Vaniah (the ancient Pennsylvania), in alliance with other religious states further west, has launched a Jihad, or holy war, against the four free counties of Ahiah (Ohio): Sandusky, Wyandot, Tuscarawas, and Mohican. In Mohican County, Ruth Jefferson McCloud, daughter of Shaker McCloud, one of the leaders of Mohican County, has grown up with three playfellows: Antony Manse, a handsome black aristocrat; her half-brother Simon Raven McCloud, who is under the influence of his grandmother the witch Faith Raven; and the hero-to-be, James George Quincy. James has been exiled mysteriously from Mohican County with his mother, Mary, and father, George; they have been living for some nine years in the ruined city of Hattan (Manhattan). At the beginning of the poem James and his mother have just escaped from Hattan Riot and are on their way eastward back to their native Ahiah.

GENEALOGY OF McCLOUD/QUINCY FAMILIES

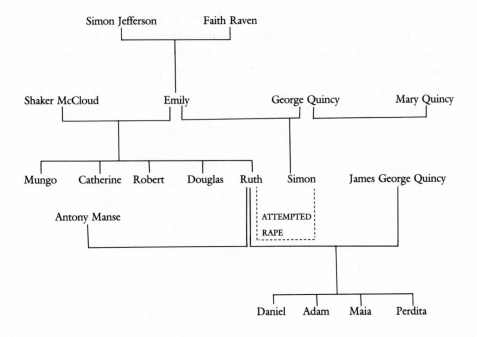

I

◆◆◆◆◆◆◆◆◆◆◆◆◆◆◆◆◆◆◆◆◆

THE HERO

The Tussen, Evitts, Wills are dark with squalls
but it's cleared in the valley, bright green farmsteads,
glassy white domes in a globe of golden light,
windvanes flashing as they turn in the freshening breeze,
rivers that glitter like foil. Being a Kshatriya,
the mother will follow her son, but in the abandon
of service, there's a sensuous impulse and self-will.
What pruning of the heart has pressed forth this fertility
of joy in her, hopeless, self-despairing as she is?
The chill returns; it thunders, and the mist rolls in.

◆

These are the Mad Counties of Vaniah which have vowed
to carry the Gospel of Christ by the force of their arms
and the fire of their knighthood to all unbelievers and heretics.
But the farms on the road, for the most part, are friendly to travelers,
recognize James George Quincy and Mary
his mother by their garments and speech to be Vates or Kshatriyas,
give them clean beds and fundamentalist food—
unsalted bean soups, braided breads, sausages,
hearty after a day's trudge in the rain.
One surly farmer picked up a stick,
muttered a curse against godless and unclean foreigners,
but fled when the boy put his hand to the hilt of Adamant.
Once on a stovetop in plain view of any
scandalized visiting minister James and his mother
saw lying a brand-new Sears Roebuck catalog,
filled with the art of a gentler civilization,
the odes and the tintings that lay on material life
its sweetness, its specious promise, to us who must die.

◆

More and more as they travel west they hear
the rumor of war. The Mad Counties, for once,
have settled their doctrinal differences, banded together
to carry the Gospel to the infidels of Ahiah.
To appease Allegany, Somerset County has banned
from its borders all Alleganian refugee snake handlers;
Allegany has grudgingly recognized the evangel ministries
of Susquehanna, Monongahela, Shamokin,

and permitted, with licences, revival camps from those ministries.
The moderate counties have vowed noninterference
bullied by Bible-belt truculence, Vanian unity.
Ahian born, the hero James and his mother,
having cast all on the turn of this uncertain voyage
—whether they'll even be welcome when they come home—
must ask if there's a home to come home to.

♦

In a Somerset inn they lodge for the night, and fall
into conversation with a Sears traveling salesman
whose name, Maury Edsel, befits his Vaisya calling.
It was he, they find, who left the offending catalog;
he insists, to their slight embarrassment, that they call him "Skip";
he's dressed in white shoes and maroon double-knits,
travels, he tells them,"over the whole of the East,
even, like here, where powered transport's forbidden;
the pickings are richer, the folk not being exposed
to the video either, which is my chief competition.
(By treaty the multinational corporations
may operate here if they pay a good tithe to the church.)
There isn't much east of Cargo I don't know about."
So they seize the prerogative granted to travelers,
ease the constraints on talk between caste and caste,
for Skip is a goldmine of news. The Mad Counties,
it seems, have given up hope of converting the Riots,
have ceased their raids on the Burbs that in terror pay tribute
to Delphia Riot and Pitsburg; have turned their attention
to the High Counties that lie to the west. They have launched
a two-pronged attack, one south of Pitsburg,
and one to the north, skirting the Kelan Riot.
They hope to take Tuscarawas County by winter,
reclaim the Amish lands, launch a full-scale attack
on Sandusky and Mohican Counties the following spring.

♦

Mohican County! will your domes and amphitheatres
fall to the torch of barbarians? Where scholarship flourishes,
strangers who come from the stars are made welcome to learn
from our craftsmen, our libraries, houses of science and music?

5

where, by our disciplines, the person is finer than otherwhere,
for the art of life is hammered here to perfection?
Mohican, mother of your poet, so powerful-seeming,
when all two hundred thousand citizens gather
yearly at the festival in Mount Verdant, when we see the cupolas
of your cathedral, after many days' travel, blaze in the sun,
you're no more than the breath of a flower in a fine globe of glass.
And all those planters, year after year, who poured
into this ground the overflowing of their spirit—
Johnny Appleseed whom we remember in our little shrines,
John Crowe Ransom, Griselda the gardener,
Bender the Shaman, Elizabeth our first praetor—
who would not eat the fruits that others offered
but chose Ahian earth, where the Mohican river
glitters, to bury wit, goodness, passion
as the poor fool buried the talent in the parable
where there was no assurance they might grow—
all of the planters, seeing their garden devoured,
must they then mourn their city without recompense?

◆

"Heck," says Skip, "you look like you've just seen a ghost."
"Mohican's our home. After nine years we're returning."
"No shit. You're in a whole heap of trouble.
Take my advice and go back. They won't mess with you here,
but out further west it's a sick elephant's toilet."
"This is a lady, Skip, so please watch your language.
We give you our thanks for the warning but we have no choice
but to continue. Some iron for your good intentions."
The boy gives him one of the last of their coins,
the resin varnish worn almost down to the iron.
Skip wraps it up gravely, records the event on his 'puter.
"That's a High Countian gift, even I can see that,"
says he. "I don't mean to be nosey, sir,
But aren't you—no offense—young to be traveling so far
in charge of the lady?" "No business of yours,
but I am seventeen and able to look after myself—"
he touches the scabbard of Adamant. "—And my mother,"
he adds, rather angrily, seeing her hide a sad smile.
"Hey, hey, no offense!" says Skip, alarmed and amused.

6

"I was going to ask, if you're bound and set to go west,
and I'm going that way, couldn't I come with you,
I mean, under your protection." "Maury Edsel,
take care. Those I protect must have no reservations
nor falseness of heart, for I will brook no betrayal.
How may I know that you are no spy or traitor?
And what do you have to offer my mother in service?"
"There isn't no way that I can prove myself honest.
Take me or leave me. But perhaps you could use some advice
on the way. Like, you know, fellow-travelers."
The young man relents. "Agreed. and please pass the pie."

♦

Of all measures of value, numerical quantity,
marked in human affairs by money currency,
most common, is also most shared. Truth, goodness,
beauty, are the flowers of refinement; in them the fire
of reality burns more fiercely, but only the few
whose hearts, like crucible ceramic, have been tested in the flame,
may know those radiances. Bless number then,
the speech the crassest nuclear iota speaks,
and money, which is the numbering of human deeds,
the telling in the common tongue, the ligaments of love.

♦

On Skip's advice they go at once into disguise.
In a shop smelling of fabric, ivory buttons,
heavy-cut cotton and dye, they purchase new clothes.
The boy puts off the cloak, tunic, and breeches
of the hero, wraps up the sword in silk, and stows it
in his pack; puts on the black suit, the vest, and tall hat
of the fundamentalist farmer. His mother, in apron and bonnet
might be come fresh from a farm prayer breakfast.
Skip stays as he is: no one will stoop
to bother a Vaisya. Thus clothed like its enemies
they strike for the embattled borders of their native land.

2. The Storytelling Game

The road now passes through gentler landscapes.
On Laurel Hill the sun comes out again,
waterdrops flash in a rayed point of scarlet
or blue; heavenly shafts through the clusters of leaves;
the wood smells of leather and skylight and soil.
On Chestnut Ridge their first signs of war overtake them:
troops heavily armed, choking the way,
methahol trucks (permitted for war, not for peace),
wains drawn by greathorses, loaded with rocketry,
food wagons, mobile microprocessor shops,
two or three highly expensive tanks
clad in their jet-black resinite armor.
Overhead can be heard the drone of sunplanes in echelon
and sometimes a hillside is darkened, a dirigible's shadow.
To ease their minds, the companions fall into talk,
and thence into stories, which always shorten the journey.
"When I was just an apprentice salesman," says Skip,
"one of the master travelers made me a wager.
He showed me a boxful of widgets he had, and bet me
a Sears traveling dealership I couldn't sell four of them.
Sears is the ace. I was only a kid. It was easy.
'You're on. What's the catch?' I asked him, street-wise.
'The catch: you must sell one to a Free Countian,
one to a Mad, one to a Rioter, and one
to a Burbian. And no lies.' He'd caught many young salesmen
that way; he had theories of human psychology, thought
he might make me a fool. But I had some theories too.
First I sought out a Free Countian, told her
in frankness all that had happened. She, being a lady,
was pleased with the game. 'The widget's expensive,' she said,
'but it's cheap if you promise to tell me the story of how
you have fared, when it's over.' I agreed. Next I approached
a Mad Countain farmer I knew, picked
for a public morality that masked a fevered desire
to know what Free Countian women do
with their men. (The preacher in Puritan districts loves
to inveigh in language so vague that nobody knows

what he means, against 'practices,' 'pleasures,' 'abominations,'
inflaming the boys' curiosity in the back row of pews.)
So I told him in private I had a device that I'd sold
only last week to a Free County woman, that she
had assured me would give her the most refined pleasure, though I
hadn't the faintest idea what she would do with it.
'But,' I said, 'I'll bet she's doing it now.'
The fellow paid me twice what I'd got from the lady.
Two widgets to go. The problem with Rioters,
when you have something to sell, is not selling
but finding something of value they haven't spent yet.
No Rioter works, as you know; work
infringes their freedom; the world owes them a living.
But Burbians work, to pay the Rioters' levies,
and sometimes keep something by between burnings and taxes.
Burbians (pardon me, Ma'am) have no balls to speak of
and Rioters scare them shitless. The Burbian Government
(which used to be called the Uess Federal Government)
is controlled by the Riots. So. I found a Burbian,
gave him a widget, and asked him to keep it safe
from the Rioters down the street; then approached a huge Rioter,
showed him a widget, told how eagerly Countians
paid for them—even that wretched Burbian had one.
Rioters know what to want by wanting what other folk
show that they want by possessing. My Rioter cornered
the Burbian, made him give over the widget I gave him.
Shocked, I called to my aid a yet uglier Rioter
and told him the story. His eyes gleamed with cunning.
'I want a widget,' he said. 'That Burbian pays.'
So the Burbian paid for the widget he wanted. But I,
ready to sting, asked the Rioters why they would want
and be willing to buy (at the Burbian's expense) a thing
that the Burbian got without paying. Struck by injustice,
the Rioters huddled, agreed that the Burbian must buy
his own widget, else it wasn't worth stealing.
So the first Rioter gave me my widget back
and taxed its replacement out of my scared Burbian.
When I told the tale to the Countian lady she laughed.
'So all six of us win at the wager: I,
with a story worth seventeen widgets; the farmer, with hours

of pleasure (though I fear you have used me most shamefully);
the Rioters too, who have got what other folk want,
even the Burbian, who has escaped with his life;
and you, who have got your Sears concession, though why
you should want such a thing is surely a mystery to me.' "

♦

"We must beware when you have something to sell,"
says James George, laughing. "A tale well told."
"Cap it," says Skip. "Don't you, Sir,
have a story to tell?" "What kind of story? I've never
told one before." "How about how you came by
the sword?" "O, the sword. Well, I might. . . ."
"James." Mary speaks for the first time.
Her face scarcely conceals her fear and her grief.
"Mother, what harm can it do? I shall say nothing
to demean the name of the Quincys." She bows her head.

♦

"For nine years we have lived in Hattan Riot.
There is in Hattan, south of Central Park
A region like no other in the world:
one that is neither County, Burb, nor Riot,
where strange folk walk among the twilight towers.
A wisdom that has broken from belief
and aged beyond the hopes of human action
lives in that place, mocking experience
with lidless eyes. But we had settled there,
my father, who was, when he lived, a master
of the sword, skilled in all ways of war,
my mother, and myself. We made a life
by teaching those who came to us the arts
of music, poetry, and single combat;
My father, whom I loved, would tutor me
in all the ways of the intelligent sword.
For every named sword, such as Adamant,
must, if we rightly honored it, be held
as a person; each of the great swords has
a tiny microprocessor, or Mike
within its hilt, that feeds upon the sun

and knows its master, and controls the weight
and balance of the sword, the flex of steel,
momentum of the blade, and hones its edge.
The molecules themselves obey the pulse
the Mike sends through them, and their crystals pack
or wander as the weapon's will inclines.
This, not the king's ransom's worth of steel,
is why a sword is held to be so precious.
When we went into exile from Mohican
I know my father carried such a sword;
but once we'd settled down, it disappeared:
My father taught me with a lesser sword.
He would be gone sometimes for many hours,
returning moody and uncertain; then one day
two months ago, father did not come back.
I searched for him, in grief and terror, but
could find no sign; at last came in despair
to the Queen Bee of Hattan Riot, Mome.
She was a beauty in a fat white way,
and by her side her son, the Slob, sat smiling.
'Where is my father?' I burst out. I knew
at once that they had taken him away.
'Down in the subways with the alligators.
Kingfish has him, if you want him back.'
'Who's Kingfish?' 'Only Kingfish know,' she said.
'Where is he, then?' Mome smiled. 'Grand Central Station.'
'But since the buildings fell the way is blocked!'
'Not if you know the subway.' 'But I don't.'
'My son the Slob has got the map,' she said.
'Give it to me.' 'You'll have to fight him for it.'
The Slob was seven feet high, four feet across,
a mountain of white fat and vapid smile.
I was insane with fear and rage. It was
a day of hazy sun. The Hattan summer
boiled under plane trees at the World Trade Center
there at the Riot's rotting nucleus.
The Slob was never taught to talk, but he
came for me wordless with a spittle strand
hung from his chin. He had a knife, but I
was not afraid of that. If he could pin me

11

he'd break me quick with his four hundred pounds.
I kicked the knife away. He groped at me;
I lashed him with my fists. He blinked, and smiled.
I hit him in the paunch; it was like dough.
Rioters jabbered in a ring around us.
Soon he would have me. What of his could hurt?
I took his right hand in my own, and squeezed.
Now a blue tear came into both his eyes.
His hand was very small. I ground my teeth
and squeezed again. There was a pop of knuckles
and veins burst in his pinkie. Now I roared
and crushed his hand with all my rage, and bent
the great arm till the elbow cracked. He screamed
and tried to flee. His skin tore from his hand,
revealed the clusters of white fat. His eyes
turned up, and like a sack of sand, he dropped.
Before his friends could move, I seized his knife
and held it to his throat. 'The map,' I said.
They brought it to me. It was red and white,
faded and worn, 'Transit Authority'
in blue. I took it, made them stand far off,
and fled at once. They would come hunting for me;
the Queen Bee would not suffer unavenged."

◆

Evening clouds, as he speaks, have come up from the west.
Under their skirts there is a rim of crimson,
five tiny cumuli swim in a bright lake of gold.
The travelers feel the first raindrops, hurry for shelter,
make their beds inside an abandoned farmhouse
that Skip knows well, close to the road on a hill.
They feast on good bread and butter, with a heel of corned beef;
Skip gets out an illegal bottle of wine.
They go to sleep early, exhausted, in separate rooms.

◆

At night Mary comes in to her son and wakes him.
She's shuddering, though it's not cold. She says not a word.
James give her his blanket, sits by a wall,
lays his arm over her shoulder. She falls asleep.

12

But now in his grief he cannot find where she's gone,
that place of forgetfulness, dreaming she is a child;
like strokes of a nightmare bell the questions return:
What was my father? What does my mother know
that I do not know? Who am I to become?
What must I hold for certain, to be what I am?—
And he closes his eyes only an hour before dawn.

3. Kingfish

In the morning they travel several miles in silence.
But Skip wants to know how the story came out.
"What did your story have to do with your sword?"
James gives a glance at his mother. She is resigned.
He is puzzled, but decides to continue nevertheless.

◆

"How to describe the caverns of that city?
Nobody sane will break the barriers
that block the undergates, lest things should issue
that thicken brave men's blood. Yet sometimes they
are opened from within, and closed again,
though for what purpose nobody can say.
But with the book I must go down and seek
the thing called Kingfish that the Queen Bee spoke of.
I took a light, but stripped off all my clothes,
for there were floods, I knew, within the deeper caves.
I wrapped the map book many times to shroud it
from the water; carried no weapon, for
my own hands and my rage seemed quite sufficient.
I broke the barricade near Fifty-eighth.
The ancient map had been corrected since
to show the cave-ins and the floodwaters:
Grand Central should not be quite a mile.
It was stark cold after the blaze of day;
the flashlight cast a little gloomy light
most like a shade. My body shivered once.

That passage was the worst I can remember.
Among the dead the rats kept festival
And once I saw a pair of lambent eyes
that dimmed and turned away before my rage.
In one place there was water to the roof
And I must swim seventy feet or more
with only rock and water over me.
At length, after many a false turning,
when my hot anger almost turned to fear,
I came to a lit chamber where I saw
wonders that still I do not understand.
There was a ringing in my ears I'd thought
to be the beating of my heart, but it
grew louder, banged like hammers, and then ceased.
There on a great chair sat an ancient man.
His face was black as charcoal and as cracked
and warped; his eyes peered through a whitish scale.
His teeth were gone, but still his arms and shoulders
seemed hale and massive like a stumpy tree.
And on his knees there lay a man. I growled,
for I had recognized Sir George my father.
I started forward. 'Come no closer, boy,'
said the old man. 'See, you cain't move a foot.'
It was the truth, for I was stricken still
as stone, must stand there till he let me go.
And now I saw upon my father's breast
a fine scabbard, and in it was a sword.
'Are you called Kingfish?' 'Dat's de name,' he said.
He shifted. 'O, de pain in mah pore ass.
Ah never get de cure. Ah knows yo' name,
boy, ain't it James? Dey call you Rollo once;
one day yo' followers will call you Jago,
'cause you will drive de heathen from de land.
And when yo' be an outlaw yo'll be "Robin";
and "George" yo' be, which be yo' father's name.'
'Why does his murderer know all my names?'
'O mah achin' ass. All de wrong questions.
Boy, ah ain't killed yo' father. He mah friend.

14

De one dey call de Slob, he kill yo' father.
Ah took him body from de Riot Queen.'
'Then I shall finish what I have begun.'
'Let him to die, boy; he be jus' a child.
Cain't feed hisself widout his arm. His maw
will t'row him out; an' he so dumb he starve.
Now yo' be sorry for de wretch, don' hate no mo'.'
'Sorry for *him*?' I cried. '*Right*. (Oh mah ass.)
He be de end-point of four hunnert years
since John Jake Rousseau and his baby, Sart,
an' all dem rebels 'gainst Eddipus
said dat we must be free. De Slob was free.
He had no law to keep him from his mamma;
no language in his haid to see hisself;
no good intentions—dey're the road to sin;
no tryin' to feel what other people feel;
no separation from his work, 'cause he din' work;
no self, no shame, no gods, no punishment;
no death; no money—Man, he *civilized*.'
'Why did he kill my father then?' I cried. . . . "

◆

Carried away by the story, James has forgotten
his mother's distress. But now he hears her sigh
and pauses. She's right. What Kingfish had said to him then
could not be repeated. "Now listen up, boy. When yo' daddy
was young as yo' is, he was restless and wanted to see
what was outside de borders of de land of Ahiah.
He foun' his way here, hearin' dat ah was a swordsmith.
He seem like a promisin' boy. Ah 'lowed ah would teach him.
Ah loved dat man; ah got as much cause as you have
to weep for him. But still he's dead by mah fault, ah know,
and when ah be done yo' can strike dis ol' white head down.
Ah tired of de years, a hunnert and forty-four.
Ah taught him too quick. Not de way of de sword
but de way of de world. Ah took him out to de edge
and he never turn round and bless de world dat he come from,
but kep' right on goin', out into de dark
where nothin' got value, nothin' got groun' underneath.
Every man got an angle, but dey all believe

15

dat dere's one great big Eye knows all de truth.
When he stop b'lievin' in de Eye he b'lieve in nothing.
Then ah got worried, tried to cosy him back,
tol' him, de angles you see it, is one of de things
dat de world is made of. He tried to believe, but inside
he was a wild boy, and de wildness turn to despair.
When ah seen what ah done ah suffered de bitter repentance;
And ah give him de finest of all of my swords, called de Serpent.
Ah hammered it out of the last of de rails in de subway.
He took it an' give it a different name, Adamant,
an' swore dat his soul would be firm as de blade dat he bore;
then he lef' to marry his Mohican sweetheart, Mary.
But when he return, nine years back,
he be broken in spirit, and he give de sword back to me
'less he lost it or sell it, 'cause he was becomin' a drunk.
He took up wid de Queen Bee, and fell in de dirt
and tried to forget what it felt to be Samurai-born.
Heaven know what he done wid dat woman. Dey sold
half of Hattan to get dem more joyjuice; I sorry to tell you
he live like a pig. But den he die like a hero.
When de Slob was growed up he wanted his maw to hisself,
'cause he was de favorite son. So he got all his brothers
and laid for de man. He was drunk, but he fought: broke
de haid of one wid a stone and strangle another.
But de Slob was behin' him and stuck him through wid a stake.
Mah Guardian Angels bring me his body las' night:
de Slob must have stolen from him de map of de subway.
Now you got yo' choice, boy. Yo' can strike me down
or leave me to live with mah pain. Ah give you de sword
which is yo' own, to do as yo' wish," he said.

◆

"What's the matter, sir? Why don't you finish the story?"
asks Skip. With a look at his mother, James continues.
"Old Kingfish was the maker of the sword.
It was my father's. Now it came to me.
Father had given it him for safekeeping.
Then Kingfish told me I must take my mother
And seek what welcome there might be at home,
Mohican County, where we now return."

16

♦

"Now that's a dandy story," said the salesman,
"But I hope you don't mind me saying—it's shot full of holes.
Why did the Slob kill your father? Why did your father
give up the sword? How did Kingfish know
your father? And why did he leave Mohican at all?"
"It's the holes in a story that make it a story," says James,
"Like the holes in the bread." He speaks lightly, but now he is sure
there is something concerning their exile that he doesn't know,
something concerning his birth. He tries to recall
the years of his childhood, those happy years on the farm
at Lithend in Mohican; but none of us knows for sure
the thing that concerns us most dearly: how we began.
For if a man makes himself, he must forget whence he came
and if he remember, he fears lest he be unmade.

4. War in the Vales

Four days; they have crossed the frontier
into Monongahela County, and now they are come
to a land of deep vales sloping westward
and war seems all about them; this country was once
a northern horn of the State of Wesjiniah but now
is contested land between the Vanian Counties
and Tuscarawas in Ahiah. The first onslaught
has scattered the screen of Ahian troops at the border
and driven them back to the river. The road now passes
down dark defiles towards the old city of Wheeling:
above the road Ahian fortresses, gutted
and smoking, stand empty of their garrisons, which have fled westward.
The Tuscarawans must have decided to hold
the crossings of the River Ahiah, and to wait for help
from their eastern allies Mohican, Sandusky, and Wyandot;
but even with those reinforcements they are badly outnumbered,
and a Mad Countian force almost as large,
the travelers hear from a Vanian soldier, broke through
to the north three days ago, crossed the river in strength.

17

the dead he had seen had not much impressed him, but now
he remembers the grass soaked with blood, the fishes
fighting each other for something in the pools of the river;
and all is smeared with a frightful smell of the unfamiliar;
and the days of childhood seem terribly close, and terribly
far away. But now Mary his mother
rides up beside him and touches his arm with her hand;
a little warmth comes into the present, he laughs
and calls to Skip to break out some bread and some wine.
They share the wholesome crust with the riders about them;
there's even enough of the coarse Cayuga Red
in the bottle to give them a swallow to keep out the cold.

◆

Later that night they halt near the brow of a hill.
The company's marshaled into a line with a wedge
at each end. Some of the riders dismount and unlimber
the rockets and tubes, with their tiny hand-held controls.
Others move forward with heavy laser equipment;
an eye drone's sent up with a whisper of displaced air.
Scouts have reported a column of Somerset infantry
with a tank support group. Someone lends Rollo
a pair of infrared cavalry glasses; he creeps
to the top of the rise and sees, issuing from a wood,
a ghostly pink line of movement; focusing closer
he can even see faces, confident, young, unsuspecting.
He goes back to his horse and loosens the sword in its sheath.
Mary and Skip will hang back with the rockets and lasers,
though it's hard for Rollo to persuade his mother to stay,
she being Kshatriya; but Skip is quaking with terror
and someone must stay to quiet his Vaisya panic.

◆

The order is given; the head of the enemy column
has passed through a bend in the valley; the first wedge
breaks into movement, crests the top of the rise,
and canters on down. Meanwhile with a scream and a whoop
the rockets rush from their tubes and converge in red cones
on the tanks, strung out among the plodding foot soldiers.
With cracks like lightning the ion paths are established

that will guide the punching pulses of laser light into
their targets; the valley floor leaps into detail and perspective
as bursts of actinic light like chrysanthemums flower
in series along the line of the road. Now
the second cavalry wedge moves over the crest,
and sweeps down the slope toward the eaves of the wood,
just as the first cuts through the neck of the column
with a roar and a dazzle of sabers, and wheels to attack
the oncoming troops strung out on the road. At last
some enemy soldiers around the two tanks
that have not been hit, begin in confusion returning
the fire. Rockets shoot from their racks on the tanks
and rush up the slopes to explode among men on the crest.
Enemy troops come pouring pell-mell from the trees.
A smell of ozone and fire drifts in the air.
But that moment the second wave strikes, cutting
the line, choking the flow of reinforcements, and setting
new panic among the Somerset men.
The segment of enemy line, a cut worm, must turn
in two directions at once, but they still outnumber
the Ahians by three to one, did they but know it.
Now the third platoon, strung out in a line,
hears the order to charge, breaks into a gallop,
thundering down the slope. Among them Rollo,
his face very white, his eyes like coals in his head,
lashes his sword from its scabbard, the hiss of a meteor,
raises his voice in the family war cry: "Aoi!"
They burst on the enemy line as surf on the breakwater
shatters in blossoms of phosphorescence and sweeps
in green tons over the wall. A moment
of shock: Rollo's sword has been horribly agile
and has danced in an omega twice to the left and the right;
each time it has found a joint in the armor;
but Rollo, armorless, has suffered a jolt in the thigh
that suddenly spasms with trickles of frightening stickiness.
Nevertheless, he turns and charges the tanks
whose lasers are now cutting systematically
into the knots of Ahians defending the flank.
But his horse, struck by the same beam as he, stumbles,
and Rollo throws himself clear as the beast somersaults.

21

He gasps with the pain, but the accident seems to him lucky:
he has fallen beside a heavy Vanian laser
abandoned amid the melee. He props it up
over the corpse of his horse, training it carefully
into the tank-visor, fires, and the tank erupts
in a blue poppy of incandescent methahol.
The shock wave lifts him up; he grunts and blacks out.

♦

It is only a few moments later. He is cold and sick.
Nearby the firing's died down. He can hear on all sides
the terrified, unpracticed complaints of humans in pain:
that animal which, with its beautifully sensitive cortex
risks the most extravagant achievements of agony.
The Christian troops, surrounded, have been forced to surrender;
close by, a Tuscarawan's disarming a group of them;
they are clearly surprised, having heard from their Elders and ministers
that the godless humanists do not stop short of murdering
unborn babies, but eat their enemies live
in orgies of drug-crazed sexual frenzy.
Rollo tries to get up. The wound in his thigh
is shallow, dealt by a bolt that glanced off the flank plate
of his horse before burning on through. He gropes for his sword,
and finding it, places his hand on the blade in gratitude:
the fierce thing hums to him, heaves itself into the sheath.

♦

There's a burst of explosions down at the edge of the wood;
the Ahians have mined it to give themselves time to escape.
The troops from the hilltop arrive, with Mary and Skip.
They release the Vanian prisoners, and order them home
with instructions to tell of the mercy and might of Ahiah.
The raiders vanish into the night, riding north
and then west to the river. It's a wild ride;
they must reach Martin's Ferry by dawn, or they're lost.

♦

At Martin's Ferry a flat-bottomed barge has been hidden
with sweeps to row it across. The raiders embark,
but just as they're pushing off, shapes appear upriver,

and they hastily warp the barge into the bushes.
The Vanian forces upstream, gaining the victory,
are sending their transports to Wheeling by night to surprise
the Ahian defenders, ferry the Vanian army
over the river and establish a western beachhead.
It's a disaster. All radio wavelengths are jammed;
the Ahian synchronous satellites were shot down by laser
in the first hours of the war: no line-of-sight.
Antony Manse and his captain confer, and decide
that all they can do is wait till the transports have passed,
cross over, and ride like the black Tornado of Yahman
to warn the army of Wheeling. Two hours to dawn.

♦

The fleet of transports seems endless. Discipline's good:
no lights can be seen. One or two muttered orders
carry over the waters ablaze with the westering moon.
At last they are gone, passing beyond a dark headland.
And now, suddenly, all of the valley appears
in the palest of monotone blue, but in depth, while the moon
which had seemed so far and so round and so bright has become
only a flat white piece of the sky.
At once they shove off, but halfway across the alarm
is sounded behind them. The Vanians open fire
but answering fire from the barge distracts their aim
and the raiders escape to the shore. As they expected
the landwire, a buried organic superconductor,
has been cut north and south. They must ride through the hills,
for the river road's far too exposed to attack from the east.

♦

Now they are all exhausted. Some of the horses
have foundered; the wounded are left in a wood with the doctor.
But a strange gaiety rises in Rollo's arteries,
for at last he feels the heart-swelling closeness of home.
As they ride on the hills, the light of Ahiah opens
and opens; they wade through flowers of the field, milkweed,
goldenrod, Queen Anne's lace, asters as purple
as zenith at evening, daisies yellow with polyanth
centers as powdery black as the night, cornflowers

23

saturate blue as the noon; honey-sweet clouds
of wild roses, speckled with cream upon white upon white.
In the woodlands the dogwoods and ivy are crimson as lipstick,
sycamores yellow as candy, or angelica green;
and whole groves of apple trees, the fruit with green cheeks
each painted with an identical scarlet daub,
and smelling as all the world's apples had breathed a cold breath.
The millions of leaves each show a distinct
heraldic trademark, complex and elegant outline,
the assertion of beechness, viburnum, hackberry, flowering
cherry, white oak, red oak, pin oak, plane.
The air of Ahiah in fall is like alcohol, white
as the water of streams, but more sharply refractive
so that edges glow with the overflowed light, and shapes
seem as eccentrically warped as they in fact are,
and the blue hills pop up over the horizon
like blue eyes opening on the first morning.

♦

And so I leave James George Quincy
with his recovered name, and his mother, and their companions in arms
riding over the hills to the battle of Wheeling;
and I turn to the fortunes of the McClouds of Wolverton Hill
in Mohican, and the chatelaine, Ruth Jefferson McCloud,
and her father the chieftain, mighty Shaker McCloud.

II

◆◆◆◆◆◆◆◆◆◆◆◆◆◆◆◆◆◆◆◆◆◆

THE HEROINE

1. Family History

There was a man called Simon Jefferson, a Mohican
who felt the call of that god whose name is Yahman.
He left his farm in the hands of his younger brother
and set out to find if his god might be better known
in the Black Counties of Vaniah. The shriek in the melody
of Black Country music, the maddening intricate designs,
without figures or representations, of their napkins and quilts,
the oneness of life under the slow clouds
of a single book, the noble antiquity of the father
at the plow, the son running behind, the mother
and daughter: all sons one son
all fathers one father, all
mothers one mother, all daughters
one—that life called him and he followed
till he came to Shamokin County, where he settled down.
There he married a woman called Faith Raven,
but being unable to consummate wedlock with her
he grew bitter, and she, losing her faith, turned to witchcraft;
but nothing availed. At last, believing that if
he returned to his home, his manhood might thus be restored,
he brought his wife back to Mohican County.
They bought a farm near Mount Verdant, and behold, she conceived
and in time gave birth to a daughter, Emily Jefferson.
But the daughter grew up wild, believing in nothing;
she was called "Long-Legs" because of her beauty and grace
and many men sought her in marriage, with little success.
Now the name of the Jeffersons' farm was Avalon, for it lay
in a valley where grew an ancient orchard of apple trees
and in the cup of the hills was a clear lake.
And one day in spring "Long-Legs" swung in a swing
her father had made in an apple tree when she was a girl,
and a tall man came riding by on a horse
greater than any she'd seen. "Who are you?"
she asked, "And where do you come from?" He replied:
"We are neighbors and should not need to make demand of names;
But I am Daniel McCloud and Wolverton Hill
is my home. Do not be surprised that you do not know me;

I have studied abroad, indeed in the stars, and returned
only ten days ago. Your name I know: it is Emily."
Later that year they were engaged to be married;
The county found them fit to be husband and wife,
awarded the privilege of children. Shaker McCloud,
as they called him, was one of the foremost persons in the county:
a man of great strength of limb, and wealth, and power,
elected a senator by the representatives of the district.

◆

Five children were born to Shaker and Emily.
The first was named Mungo: he was a tall fellow
with fair hair and a long face; he loved
riding and hunting, and to be a fine figure
in the County. When he was twelve he went off to school,
as is the custom, but did not do well in his studies;
he was clever enough to keep his County scholarship
but spent his time with the foolish and braggart boys.
One day he was caught cheating on an exam,
not on his own behalf but to help one of his friends,
a popular and lazy youth, and was expelled from the school;
his father Shaker, who had indulged him, was angry;
the boy had never taken an interest in the farm,
and when the time came for him to receive his portion,
Shaker offered no land, but only money,
that is, a share of the County's obligations to the family.
Emily loved him, and gave him the choice between land
and money, but Mungo chose money and went on his way.
Later he married the daughter of Claudius Manse,
whose name was Celia Manse and who was well matched to him
in fortune and temper; this Celia was the sister
of Antony Manse, who led the Mohican raiders.

◆

A year after Mungo was born, Emily conceived
and gave birth to a daughter, Catherine; she was her father's
favorite; grew up beautiful, black-haired, spoiled.
Catherine had second sight, and often her dreams
came to pass. She could turn Shaker her father

about her little finger; he would take her up
on his knee, and make her tell one of her wise little stories.
One night she dreamed a dream: the old ram
of the flock fell sick, and a great black bird
flew down and pecked out his eyes. Out of his body
there sprang a black lamb; and the bird fed
the lamb till he became mighty. And again she dreamed:
that her mother Emily had a ring that she loved, but she lost it,
but then one day when she was eating an apple
the ring fell out where Shaker could see it; but she
fell sick of the apple. And once again she dreamed:
that there was a king who was slain by a boar in the forest;
but a great eagle came down, and slew the boar.
Cathy was only a child of seven when she dreamed
these dreams, and nobody knew what was their meaning;
but next winter Simon Jefferson fell sick,
though none of the doctors could find anything wrong,
and he vomited, shrieked, and begged that he might be released.
He recovered; was well for a while but fell ill again,
and then once again. And fearing lest the affliction
return, he took his own life. People remembered
that Faith, his wife, was surnamed Raven, that she hated
her husband for carrying her into Ahiah; it seemed
that she was the black bird of Catherine's dream.
After that Faith lived by herself at Avalon,
the farm in the valley of apples, and was feared as a witch.
But Catherine grew, and her father loved her and wished
that she should inherit Wolverton Hill. But she,
like Mungo, had no patience for the cares of a farm,
of service to County, allies, councils, and feasts.

◆

Next after Catherine a son was born, Robert;
Until he was three years old he was wild and unruly,
but thereafter was sweet and mild and was loved by everyone;
and his thoughts dwelled with the divine, and the goodness of man
that redeems him; he worshiped especially that god named Sperimenh,
Healer; when he came of age he renounced all property
and shaved his head, and was a holy priest,
and he joined an order of monks, and his name was Siddhartha.

29

And then came a third son, whom they named Douglas;
he had a quick wit and sandy hair, and loved
to make people laugh; soon he began to write poetry,
and in it he praised the good wine of the Wolverton slopes
and the cheese and timber and fine woolen cloth of the farm;
he was clever with his hands, and learned to repair the sun cells,
the stills, and the windmills; he loved commerce, and travel,
and the talk of the markets; one day he met a merchant
under the ensign of the great house of Westinghouse
who was bound for Diana, and Noy, and Souri, and west
over the Counties of the Plains; he came to his father
and begged him to give him his portion that he might become
a Vaisya and travel to Calyforny; Shaker
reluctantly gave him his blessing, and Doug was apprenticed
the merchant's junior partner; together they bought
a great yellow trading dirigible, and in spring
sailed away. Doug's songs and advertisements
and adventures in love were sung in many a clime.

♦

There's a dark threshold in every human soul,
between the dawn man and the dawn woman.
It is a high crime against nature to be human
And each of us must offer in our lives the sacrifice of silencing
the inner opposite to our outer public form.
But the white ballot of awareness passes from one
to the other, and its comings and goings cannot be known
or constrained. May Pan, who presides over such transformations,
grant that his poet—hers, for Pan is androgyne—
might step by the light of day in the world of woman
and faithfully follow the sweet currents of she-words
that wind like braids in the stream of the mother tongue.
The last daughter born to Emily McCloud
was Ruth. Ill luck attended her birth. Emily
was weary of children; her daughter Catherine had stolen
a great part of her husband's affection, and her father
about this time fell sick of the witchcraft,
and presently ended himself. Shaker McCloud
that winter went off to war in the North, and Emily
fell in a fever, and sang, and then became silent,

and stayed in the family house in Mount Verdant, leaving
the child with a sweet-hearted nurse called Barbara Blubaugh.
For a while she seemed to regain her former happiness,
and when Shaker returned she was again with child.
When she saw Shaker she knew again how she loved him;
and though the baby was three weeks overdue
she kept it secret, and gave birth to a handsome boy.
He was black-haired, and had already cut a tooth,
and they called him Simon, after his dead grandfather.
And in that year Antony Manse was born;
and the next year, the hero James Quincy.

◆

But few attended Ruth, though she smiled sweetly,
but for Barbara the nurse; she was almost a stranger
in her own home, for the chief regard fell upon Simon.
But Ruth had very bright eyes, and a will of adamant,
and a pale face, and a cloud of fiery red hair.
And she learned early not to cry when she wished,
and she crept where Shaker read to the family at evening
from Dante, and Shakespeare, and Yeats, and Eleanor Palomon,
and Bender the Shaman, and Homer, and Geoffrey Chaucer,
Milton and Marlowe and Hopkins, and the poet of Gawaine,
and the Bible and Gilgamesh, Dickinson, Austen, and Rabelais,
Eschenbach, Plato, Virgil, and sweet Murasaki,
Melville and Merrill and Sappho and Keats and the Singers
of Njal and of Beowulf, Krishna and Thomas the Rhymer;
and Tolstoy, Marion Evans, Sidney, and Swift.
Ruth would follow her father's finger as he recited,
and when she was three years old she could read.
Then she turned to biology, physics, philosophy;
when she was ten she burned through the magical fever
of high mathematics, and learned of the icy pause
of geometry, that supervenes at the zenith of the mind's trajectory.
She loved her father's library, her mother's laboratory;
her fingers flew over the keys of the organ, the stops
of the viola; and her tongue grew liquid around the syllables
of Latin, Greek, German, and old Magellanic.
But when she was eleven everything changed once again.
For Faith, the old witch, in her bitterness turned against Shaker

because, she believed, he'd taken her daughter away;
She begged to come back to Wolverton Hill; was received
and presently cast Emily into a little sickness
and sat by her bed, and nursed her, and asked many questions;
and at last Emily told her that Simon her son
had been begotten upon her not by her husband
but another; but this man she would never name.
In the evil grief of her heart Faith came to Shaker
and told him what she had learned; Shaker fell down
in a swoon, and blood burst from his ears, but at length
he awoke and told his mother-in-law that he
would never speak nor act upon what she had said,
and that she must not tell Emily aught of their speech.
But Faith, thwarted, now returned to her daughter
who was swiftly recovering out of her strange sickness,
told her that Shaker knew everything, begged her to come
with her back to Shamokin County. But Faith's plans
had failed, for Emily, being a High Countian
Samurai, turned her face from her mother and fetched
a slim knife from her bosom and slew herself there
on the great blue quilt she'd made for their marriage bed.

◆

Remembering Catherine's dream of the ring and the apple,
in his rage and grief Shaker sent Faith back to Avalon
forbidding her ever return; Simon was renamed
Simon Raven, and given to Faith to raise,
for Shaker could not endure him, whom he'd loved as a son.
Simon laid up his exile forever in memory
and came to hate Shaker, as was not hard
under the teaching of Faith the witch his grandmother.
That was the year Mary and George Quincy
went away to Hattan Riot with their son,
Rollo, whom Ruth had played with in the cornfields of Lithend.

◆

Now Shaker mourned a year but found in Ruth,
his daughter, a comfort where he had least expected it.
His other children, as I have told, were growing
away from Wolverton Hill, and though he loved Cathy

he knew she was not for managing acres and men.
So the youngest became in his heart the heir of his body
and he leaned on her now as an old apple tree will lean
on its prop. And Ruth went on weaving and weaving the web
of her learning, and now above all with the threads of the Law,
for it was the meaning of human action she sought
through the maze of the past and all the decisions of men
that we dwell in as spiders inhabit the webs they have made.
But each time she unwove the pattern and so let it fall
in a rain of tears about her, for no knot sufficed
to hold the whole where the grief of her mother's death
might be weighed, compensated, assuaged. And one thing lacked:
She would always have it there must be no frontier
where the dark wind of chance, the black bird
of bad luck, might enter to tear the delicate fabric;
but no weaving so close can cover the world.
But I, your poet, am caught in the very same trap
as our heroine; that this tale I weave might be complete
I must fill in the matter of Ruth's investigations
and tell of her studies in history, policy, arts,
and the law, and set down in words, as if seeing not once
but twice, the glittering, volatile substance of life
here in this world and this strange corner of time.

2. Education: Legal History

Ruth wintered in Mount Verdant those years
though Shaker mostly stayed out at the farm. Picture her
in her long scarf of purple and white, the colors
of Mohican University, her big grey greatcoat,
pink cheeks and bright eyes, boarding
the little wooden tram crammed with students
twice her age, to take the famous lectures
of Professor Basileus on Constitutional History;
or at the Hill Playhouse before *Hamlet, Lear,*
The Birds, As You Like It, or *Agamemnon*;
or *Mohican Carnival*, or *The Magic Flute*; or afterwards

at the Gay Street Coffeehouse, over torte
and expresso, arguing theology with the graduate students;
or at the Allthing, caucusing with the Tory opposition,
fighting for increased deflation of obligation currency;
or at the crowded neo-mythologic opening
at the Hyperborean Gallery; or, her blazing hair
blown by the damp fall wind, waiting
on the cobbled apron of the little Mohican spaceport
to board the egg-shaped shuttle, and make the connection
with the Altair liner, for the expensive *Wanderjahr*
her father gave her in reward for her first degree;
or, after the wild all-star game when Mohican
upset Bluegrass in the Eastern football final,
talking a drunken Antony Manse, who was quarterback,
out of trying to steal a Keystone Kops helmet
off the kop who was wearing it; or on her knees in the nave
of Pan in Mount Verdant Cathedral, under its domes
of blown glass and oakwood cupolas and minarets,
praying that she might learn to share the mysteries—
butter and apples and wine—of that jolly god Pan.

◆

Machines. Once it was thought they were the mainspring
of history, that human arrangements derived from the means
of production, that class, caste, money—yes, art,
worship, the forms of philosophy—turned, epicycles,
driven by the great wheel of techne, of mechanism.
That theory itself was a machine, devised
by men to satisfy wishes invented by men
and abolished, if fashion so favored, by the same fantasy.
It served for a while our lust for metaphysical unity;
in its day it did indeed govern many events
and long after it died men invoked its authority.
This was the first thing that Ruth learned about history:
that desire drove the strange trajectory of the world,
and desires were made and unmade by a human art.
How might one know the desires of the past, that mystery
as far beyond our immediate sight as the skin
of the retina, that vessel we see with but do not see?
Desires leave a fossil, a petrified form we may study:

the law. Laws are the frozen, heroic frescoes
of the fought-out wars of desire. We may know by the law
two classes of human desire: the desires
we desire to abolish with a Thou Shalt Not,
which we find by pouring the bronze of deductive reason
into the laws' honeycomb, losing the wax
to reveal the shape of forbidden impulses; the other
class of desires is discovered by seeing the law
as frozen intention, wish set into stone.
And laws die, because like the desires they embody
their success undoes them: hunger seeks its own death.
Accordingly Ruth set out to study the history
of the Uess Supreme Court in its last centuries.

♦

Perhaps the deepest decision the Court arrived at,
and the most far-reaching, was to confirm in the late
nineteen-seventies the legality of abortion on demand.
Together with those decisions that allowed euthanasia,
and others permitting experiment on human tissue,
it constituted a redefinition of what
it is to be human. It was no longer enough
to be historically human, that is, descended
from human progenitors. Nor was it material that the body
be live, and genetically human, and even complete.
What came to be known as "significant brain activity"
was now the criterion; the court split on the meaning
of the word "significant," split again, and at last
defined it as meaning the capacity of social intercourse.
Human, then, is as human does: to be human
means to be part of a human society, giving
and taking, effectors defining the persons of others,
receptors allowing the self to be defined by others.
The soul was legally real, but synthetic, composed
by its culture and in turn composing the culture about it.

♦

Perhaps as important were the decisions concerning
the status of minors. That "all men are created
equal" seemed not to apply to children, unless

"equality" lost the political—not to say social
and economic—meanings it gained in two hundred years
since the Framers sat down to construct a rational universe.
The landmark series of cases where children sued
for malpractice, and won, against parents and schools was only
the start of a process that, given the new definition
of Man, shattered the reigning liberal tyranny.
The children were suing for loss of their right to a soul;
forced to choose between the act of requiring
the parents to take out a bond to ensure financial
responsibility, or setting government standards
for the right to have children, the court plumped for the latter:
only the rich could afford the enormous settlements,
and the Court could not confine to the wealthy the right
of reproducing the species. But the opposite happened
in the field of public education. Just as the parents,
dazed by the narcissistic urge of the age
away from service and toward the illusory image
of self-fulfillment, had by their neglect and indifference
laid themselves open to suit by their offspring, so the schools,
up to their gills in the ordure of specialization,
a cosy berth for the bureaucratically minded,
had turned out a whole generation of bored illiterates.
But the punitive damages broke the Federal system
of schools; an army of jobless administrators
was turned out into the streets. Children, instead,
were provided with vouchers to go to what schools they would,
and a thousand splendid and various educational
foundations sprang up, some of the best bought
from the system by the teachers themselves with loans from the government.
The degree in Education died and nobody mourned it,
and the vouchers bore the legend *caveat emptor*.

◆

It was in the matter of voting that things came
to a head. For since the mark of a man had changed
from the simple natural law of genetic inheritance
to the nearly infinite variety of personal culture,
the meaning of "one man, one vote"
had changed in accordance. One could be more or less

of a man, as the degree of one's stake in and contribution
to society varied. "Half a man, half
a vote" followed with deadly impeccable logic.
Now the denial of franchise to children, long practiced,
had at last its own rationale. Worse still,
in the case of *Smith versus the United States*,
a class-action suit, the Court found itself forced
to rule that the Mint, by increasing the money supply
without a Congressional vote to increase the taxes
(for incomes inflated up into higher tax brackets)
according to the old revolutionary maxim
"no taxation without representation"
had committed, on executive order, the crime of forgery.
This decision focused attention once more
on the grievances voiced by the thirteen original colonies;
and a further suit claimed that the tax and the vote
must be proportionate one to the other, if justice
were to be served. The Court, helpless, concurred.
"Equal" had now been whittled back to what
it meant at first: equal before God
and the law. But by now the old rules of thumb
to determine a just inequality were all overthrown,
the good with the bad: race, sex, age;
merit, achievement, excellence of birth or wit;
rank, education, wealth, and class.
Where there is no inequality that even claims
to be just, unjust inequality strides naked
over the land. There are worse things than hypocrisy.
The Union, as we shall see, began to dissolve.

◆

Meanwhile, under the pressure of cases stemming
from prison reform, forensic theory was altering.
In *Gilmore versus the State of California*
a prisoner claimed his state-appointed attorney
had talked him into a plea of insanity, sending him
into a home for the criminally insane. As an inmate
he had none of the rights of a human prisoner, and even
his life before his trial had by fiat become
the life of an animal. He claimed his crime for his own,

and asked for punishment, rather than rehabilitation.
The Court sided with him and dismissed the psychologist,
arguing anyone asking for punishment knew
what was the meaning of crime. To be a person
meant to be free; and "free" meant "responsible," not only
for good acts but crimes; but a crime was only a crime
if it merited punishment. Failure to punish denies
the civil rights of the person that make him a person.
And other cases struck down the rest of the liberal
penology: imprisonment could no longer be justified
on the grounds of protecting society, for the penalty thus
would precede the probable crime, and the innocent suffer
before he incurred his guilt. The deterrent effect
was likewise invalid to justify criminals' suffering,
their pains being paid on behalf of another's temptation
to crime, or for a future crime of their own.
Society had the right to revenge, which it waived;
so all that was left was the ancient doctrine of punishment.
But no one could be compelled to undergo punishment,
all of the other threats being invalid;
and thus the unrepentant could only be freed as outlaws.

♦

These decisions, it now became clear to Ruth, had created
the new class known as the Rioters. Those
who ignored or evaded the tests for the right to have offspring;
who could not meet the parental malpractice settlements,
who paid no taxes and therefore lost the vote;
who refused to be punished and vanished out of the law—
those, the wretched who gave up their claim to humanity,
became the internal barbarians of civilization,
a horde without incest taboos, barely able
to speak, preying on others, a violent matriarchy.
But perhaps it would be foolish to pity the Rioters.
After the Great Two-Century War
against the middle class that began in Russia
with the revolution of 1917, spread
to Germany, China, Cambodia, and a century later
all over Europe, Africa, Latin America,
finally burning through much of the Uess itself—

after that war the Rioters found themselves in command,
seized hostage populations of middle-class workers
which came to be known as the Burbs, and declared themselves free.
Burbian pharmacology, under the Rioters' pressure,
synthesized joyjuice, the perfect chemical psychedelic.
Nonaddictive, it induced in the taker a pleasure
exceeding the sweetness of orgasm as a blowtorch a candle,
but also the sense of high joy, of noble passion,
long-sought achievement, comfort and rest after effort,
deliciousness, relaxation from tension, esthetic delight.
It was sure-fire and never wore out, caused
no debility but for a slight pleasant tipsiness.—
Burbian scientists gave the drug to their masters.
"Consider," Professor Basileus murmured one day
to his class, "perhaps it is we who are dupes, and they
who have found at last the meaning of human existence.
Let us ask ourselves why we do not use the drug:
our answer will be the principles of all our philosophy."

♦

And the remnants of those who still honored the contract—
children of Rioters wanting the chance to make
their own souls, a few Burbians less afraid
of freedom than of the comfortable timid bondage
of life in the Burbs, and the descendants of those who through guile
or defense had escaped the massacres, banded together
to found the Free Counties. As the Union dissolved,
an empty travesty of government lingered in Washington,
a bureaucracy endlessly given to meaningless ceremony:
and even now there exists, we are told, a President,
Congress, and even a National Defense, its forces
frozen forever in the great electronic deadlock
of 2072. "But we have digressed,"
said Professor Basileus. One more group
of crucial decisions came out of the Court in those years:
they concerned the separation of Church and State.
After the successful challenge to prayer in the schools,
the Court was faced with the task of defining religion.
To be consistent it ruled that secular humanism
was itself a religion: thus failure to pray or perform

religious rites was itself a religious practice.
There was no neutral ground. The only solution
was to demand that *all* religious observances
were to take place in the schools; to choose one was unfair
and none was impossible. This principle was commuted
in practice to teaching and praying in at least four
distinct religious traditions, including perhaps
secular relativistic humanism. The burst
of religious genius that followed was one of the glories
of human civilization. But the strictest believers—
Fundamentalist Christians, Orthodox Jews, Jehovah's
Witnesses, Communists, Nazis, Islamic Puritans—
could not endure the frightful wind and light
of the multitudinous spirit of human belief,
could not accept the beautiful unbearable tragedy
that all faiths are true. In the early years
several whole religious sects, man,
woman, and child, committed mass suicide.
But most of them turned away from the world less violently,
setting up theocratic states of their own,
and became what we now call the Mad Counties
or sometimes Black Counties because of their clothing.
But we have inherited the great religious renaissance
that in turn gave birth to the syncretistic faith
of the Counties: we know it as the Way of the Garden.
To Mohican County belongs the honor of claiming
Bender the Shaman who led us the first steps
of the Way. "But it would be wrong," said Professor Basileus,
"to claim that the law is the cause of religious history:
rather, the law is a sensitive seismograph, reading
the tremors that alter the earth. Or better, the law
is the final arena where faith can meet with its enemies."

◆

Meanwhile the great assault on the realm of heaven
had gone on; the human diaspora followed the rim
of the universe outwards, as epistemological physics
foresaw: Faster Than Light is no paradox
if you can vary the relative speed of time.
Space does not exist: there are only greater

or lesser densities of physical information.
The Mizushima-N'swanan'dongu Effect
predicts that, in terms of classical physics, the attainable
"speed" increases according to the product of the squares
of the rarefaction and distance of organized matter.
In effect, information creates its own space,
or all informations are equally spaced from each other.
It's an extension of quantum electrodynamics:
the release of energy tends to destroy information,
speed in a built-up area tends to kill children;
to go between stars is easy; between villages, hard.
"So here on this planet of ours," said Professor Basileus,
"we must creep like the tortoise in order not to destroy
the structures of information we live in; but out there,"
he gestured, "nobody minds how fast we might go,
for there's nothing important to break. And that's what we found
when we went into 'space': nothing important, nothing
to get in our way. Things only got interesting again
when we settled on planets, started a culture, and thickened
the space around us into our comfortable human
exotic civilized broth. Though still," he said,
"those great technological empires are to our taste a smidgeon
provincial. The reason I raise all this is in order
to point out the one truly important effect
of Diaspora, a nice legal desideratum:
that is, whatever we do here, this isn't
the only chance for mankind. Comparing ourselves
with all previous generations of human society,
we can afford to live in a most irresponsible
fashion—indeed, we need not be tentative, adult,
or guilty, but madcap, serious, going for broke.
When a species radiates, then it can breed new varieties,
increasing genetic risk while improving the odds,
if you take what I mean," said Professor Basileus vaguely.

3. Education: Economy

In Thirteen Hundred one might not have known that the world
might ever be governed otherwise than by barons and emperors.
That strange virus, the idea of the nation state
was in the cells, but unseen. By Two Thousand
no place on earth was unclaimed by a nation state
but a new virus was working within the blood,
and two centuries later the nations had vanished.
Soviet Russia broke into ethnic groups
and then, again, into Patriarchates. Japan
split on the lines of the great industrial families
but kept, as they had through Shogunates, co-prosperity
spheres, warlords, democracy, every conceivable
fashion of strife, the hereditary office of Emperor.
China split on linguistic and family lines,
India upon the varieties of religious belief.
Europe became for a while a single huge Riot,
but divided at last into Boroughs whose boundaries followed
the catchment areas of major-league soccer teams.
The African tribes had never lost their cohesiveness:
when the nation states fell few noticed the difference.
In Latin America nationalism survived
for a while, but dissolved under the fierce corrosion
of racial, religious, and economic separation.
In this period the Marxist/Capitalist theory
of value collapsed; as the world stared at its hands
red with the blood of the middle class, it rejected
forever the bloody doctrines of economic determinism,
economic justice, and class struggle. Meanwhile
it was the civilizations of Asia that burned
with the hottest fires of art, genius, and taste:
and with the publication of Zoemon's *Caste*
and the triumphant success of its theory in Japan and India,
much of the world adopted its principles, translating
them into the local social vernacular. In China
the study of family history by Kung-Hsu and Zhang
revealed that the best predictions of personal character,
achievement, and values were based on family background,

independent of genes, economics, race, or religion.
The true history of the human race was therefore
family tradition. Suddenly it was the mothers
who stood revealed as the great forces of history.

◆

Ruth took these two principles—caste and family—
and added a third—the new economics of value—
and from them derived the basis of Mohican society.
It was the work of Shelley Hyde that exploded
the labor theory of value. The first gift
is the freshly laid turd trustingly placed by the child
in the hand of its mother: the gift produced without pain
from the innermost self, offered in the Eden before
art, alienation, repression, and sacrifice.
The mother's disgust can produce one of two responses:
fixation in rage and deceit—the child labors
in a cynical dudgeon, an agonized, cold ingenuity
to devise a gift which, full of his angry suffering,
but disguised to please his mother's fastidious tastes,
will be found acceptable, buying a love that the self
itself did not merit. The child comes to believe
that the pain of labor is what makes value valuable,
and since value's a smothered curse, then things of value
are evils, not goods. This stunted and anguished belief
became, for a time, in the Marxist/Capitalist era
the accepted foundation of all economics: the Labor
Theory of Value. The workers, then, were cast
as the angry heroic children of wicked parents
and work was defined as wearisome slavery under
the whip of exploiters. Money, moreover, as stored
and abstracted labor, was the greatest evil of all
and was therefore desired with a terrified frenzy in order
to keep it out of the hands of others. The Marxist/
Capitalist answer was to force the mother to keep
the original gift and never to burden the child
with the soul, the light of impartial intelligence, the joy
of work, and the intricate, beautiful skill of love.
That answer created the Riots, whose mothers care not
what becomes of their children, nor whether food or a turd

is put in their mouths, and make no distinctions of grammar
or incest or property. But there was another response
that the child might make to the bind that its mother, fearful
with hope, has offered the child in return for its gift,
the bind that binds us with loving religious ligaments:
it was to laugh, and make its first joke, and thus
to arise out of the darkness of bestial solipsism
into the tragic and dazzling air of human communion:
to take wing on unfamiliar muscles, to find
in the art of discovering what will please another
the door out of the self, and therefore the threshold and shape
of the self, and the self's freedom. From that moment,
taken rightly, as the two eyes amazingly cross
and form out of a maddening contradiction of views
the impossible wholeness of three-dimensional depth,
comes the work and the art of a life, and the value that drives it.
The work of creating a proper substitute gift
is no alien task imposed from above
but the proper employment of a person making herself
as she makes what she gives to another. The acceptable gift
is fertile, and generates others: the receiver in gratitude
gives in turn, and so a community comes
into being, bound by threads of gratitude, generalized
as obligation and given material form,
to aid the weak and fallible human memory,
in money currency. And money preserves the comic
uncertainty lodged in its origins: that is why money
is funny, and does not itself make a good gift.
The Obligation Theory of Value redeems
the material world by knowing it truly as striving
toward that greater complexity known as the spirit;
work becomes the privilege given to those
who are happy; the worker becomes the parent, and all
authority a wry and blessed condition of sacrifice.
Economic wealth no longer seemed like a crime
but an honor; power was made, not seized or imposed;
value created by art, and the only means
of production, the art and power of intelligent love.

◆

At least, that was the theory: in practice, as people
inevitably must, we inhabit a muddle of motives,
misunderstandings, comic reversals, griefs
that can drive us insane. But at last after three hundred years
we had hold of a theory that did not directly attack
the meaning and beauty of all human life, and was based
on the health of the soul, not its sickness. In an exchange
of money for goods, payment consisted no longer
in the transfer of money, but the transfer of goods. Freed
from the suspicion that divided the old economic classes,
the Counties evolved hierarchical structures of mutual
respect and obligation, bearing in mind the success
of the system of caste as refined by the Asian cultures:
the Brahmins or Flamens or Vates or Shamans or Priests;
the Kshatriya-Samurai caste; the farmers or Shudras,
and the commercial caste, the Vaisyas, the heirs to the fragments
of the twentieth-century world business market.
Brahmins and Vaisyas normally do not own land;
Kshatriyas make up the bulk of the army and government.
Any citizen may declare a change in his caste
but rarely will do so after his thirtieth year,
it being hard to adapt to a new code of manners,
values, and skills. The old form of employment
vanished, for now the law required that anyone
taking up service be made a partner in the enterprise.
Land which has not been worked for five years
by its owner and partners reverts to public property
and a landless person may legally homestead upon it.
At the end of each year obligations are canceled, one
for one, by requiring an equal contribution of money
from every citizen, of whatever age or sex.
Those who don't pay are not entitled to vote
unless another contributes on their behalf.
The welfare system consists of the whole population,
for every citizen must by law give board
and lodging to anyone needing it, to be reimbursed
by the government. Every year the entire population
of Mohican County (except for a rotated crew
of essential custodians) gather within the stadium
outside Mount Verdant, where plays, essential debates,

elections, fetes, and honorable awards take place.
The two hunded thousand people elect two thousand
local electors, who choose twenty chieftains
or senators, serving a four-year term and naming
one of their number as Praetor every four years.
The two parties, Tory and Whig, command
vigorous local support and fight the elections.
The electors supervise local government, health,
education, the militia, the census. Government revenue
consists in the equal contribution of all the voters
and cannot fall short of expenditures. Every child
gets an equal share of the budget for education
as a token current in any accredited school.
Health care follows the same kind of system,
and the small professional army of Kshatriyas, expected
to furnish their own gear and weapons, are honored equally
by shares in the pool of general obligation.
On the death of a landowner her land may be inherited
by whomever she chooses, but all obligation to her
must cease, and the money returned to the pool whence it came.
Though the law ignores the sexual lives of its citizens,
marriage is only permitted to those who have proved
their qualifications in searching tests, and the right
of reproduction is only given to marriage,
and no marriage may be dissolved within
the youngest child's minority, on pain of punishment.
All legal punishments are borne voluntarily,
and must include restitution of damage and property,
but those who refuse become outlaws, their goods confiscated,
their children put up for adoption; or are permitted with honor
to end their own lives by the sword in ritual suicide.

♦

In the last spasm of primitive industrialization
the Earth's usable ores were exhausted, its fuels
consumed, and much of its people dispersed to the stars.
Third Wave industry, based on electronics,
solar and wind power, microprocessors, chromosomes,
resins, superconductors, glass, and biomass,
was the technological voice of the urge to separatism.

Each family farm is virtually independent,
catching the sun, like a tree, with silicon leaves:
storing the will of the wind in organic batteries;
growing its silicon wafers according to detailed
instructions supplied by a hand-held World Library
stocked with Shakespeare and Bach and nuclear physics;
tossing a crop of supercane into the vat,
tapping out methahol to feed the mutated urchin-grown
turbines that, raised in the fish tank and impregnated
with resinite, power the bikes, the plows, and the harvesters.
Yet despite the independence of Shudras and Kshatriyas
there's a demand for Vaisya products, for their style and beauty:
the old distinction between art and technology's gone,
and so too that between poems and advertisements.
Matter, being only a weaker dilution of spirit,
cannot tyrannize over its very own essence.
The only mass production's done by machines;
much that was once thought to be part of the future
can indeed be given reality—gadgets and gizmos—
but nobody bothers, for no Free Countian
will work on what bores him, and metal is very expensive.
Few tune in to the blizzard of self-expression
that jams the airwaves with junk from the Riots and Burbs;
Countian life and art are more entertaining.
Across the Uess the almost incomprehensible
riches of County civilization comes in
by superconducting cable: the mystical cuisine
of Loosiana, the fado-like songs of the hills,
the dance of Nuyahk, romances and plays from the Plains.
Each caste supports its characteristic
culture of arts and sciences: Vaisyas the vigor
of technical magic, mirth, and commercial song;
Shudras the live tradition, decorated by the fringes,
of the old folk, whose trunk is harder than stone;
Kshatriyas the high awareness of tragic paradox,
Mozart and Aeschylus, architrave, weapons, and wine;
Flamens the white rose of heavenly wisdom
as the novice learns to turn and bless the world he has left.

4. Education: Religion, Art, War

Mohican theology worships three gods
who oppose one another in an eternal enmity:
Pan, Yahman, and Sperimenh. Pan is the God
of Being: the world is He, and the best of all possible.
Pan divides Herself with all the fecundity
implicit in myth and the quantum seething that boils
on the surface of perfect nothingness, splitting it out
into particles paired with antiparticles: Pan
is all polytheisms, all pastoral rapes
by the river of time that, sadly reflected on both
faces of some languid ripple, propagate images.
Pan is the bull-headed beast at the primitive core
of the brain's labyrinth, the reckless drunkenness of life.
Pan is a bulging sphere of lace, whose substance is
probability itself, whose stems are the past and whose tips
are the present, exploding outwards as fast as it can,
which defines the mysterious speed of the process of time.
That absence in which the world-supersphere expands
is Yahman, the God who is named by denial and negation.
Yahman is that which we worship when in mourning the death
of one that we love, we feel for a moment lightened
and terrifyingly glad. Yahman is cold,
absconditus, dark night of the soul, the place
where we go when we step outside of ourselves, the scourge
of the senses, the white rasp of fire that rips away
touch, color, taste, sound, smell,
and swallows itself in its own aching eternity.
Yahman's the blackness that quickens the Black Counties,
the death of hope that rises again as despair,
the act's vertigo over the brink of the future,
the silence and chill of thought, when the heart's furnace
is quenched and the light has gone out. Oh, but Sperimenh,
loved in Mount Verdant as Athena was worshiped in Athens,
sweet god of humanity, what shall I say
of you? We know you as Sabbath-bride, Jesus, Krishna,
Hermes Psychopomp, Aesculapius Healer.
Virgin Mother, moon-voyager, bud-

tip, tide-turn; cambium, cortex
of the world where muteness blossoms as speech; joker
in the pack, dancer on graves, Ptah the Artist,
lover and mistress, most terrible guardian of childbirth,
intelligence dawning in light in a baby's blue eye.
Presence of presence, gift of gifts, Sperimenh,
spirit of science, questioner, Quixote, Parsifal;
Spike, spoke, prosperity, speech, esperance;
experiment, mensch, meaning, manifestation.

◆

And Ruth stood in an apse of Mount Verdant Cathedral
and saw how Mohican architectural forms
had grown from its art of belief as the branch and the leaf
from the seed, and the limb and the eye and the brain from the spiral
fleshpit crouched in the womb. Daedalus Brown
the master builder had wrought out of beautiful timber
three aisled and vaulted naves, sprung
with entasis to carry the eye to the center, and piered
with pearly white stone that became by degrees the bone
of milkwooded trees: the naves met in a lambda
of one hundred and twenty degrees, like a chemical
bond, and a burst of arches supported the thrust
of the gigantic hexagonal drum pierced with lunettes
and crowned with the glorious dome, a hundred and twenty
feet wide, blown by the Feirstein Process out of
a dazzling melt of silicon glass, a single
bubble of light, with a white rose dyed
in the heart of the glass iridescent. Around the hub
there flourished a crowd of semi-domes, sectioned cupolas
and six pagodas or minarets to anchor the dome.
The three naves were sacred to Pan, Yahman,
and Sperimenh; each opened into a dome of its own,
Pan's being rich with images, animal, leafy,
Yahman's as black as the night sky, and Sperimenh's
dancing with golden and pink figures of lovers
and heroes and clowns and sages and artists and saints.
At the heart of the structure, under the dome's apogee
was an unfenced pit, dug, it is said, a mile
into the earth, and above it, floating a foot

above floor level, a simple ceramic sculpture
of a human being of indeterminate sex
yet of a beauty belonging and touching to both.
The figure is falling; its face and body express
an uttermost grief. It hangs by the thumb on a thread
of gold from the eye of the dome, two hundred
and forty feet over one's head. Sometimes
it swings with a period slow as the change of a cloud
and shows the spin of the world by its arc of precession:
sometimes it hovers, caught in a strange free fall,
for here, where the three gods meet, is the field
of tragic suspension, the fate and glory of human
existence, whose work it is to unite, for a moment
that passes away, the three worlds of the spirit.
This is our election, and no god can replace us.

◆

Much of Mohican domestic building is based
upon blown-glass technology, sandstone, and timber,
the white oak, maple, and beech being prized
for the delicate forms they assume when carved, the red oak
and black oak, with dense purple wood, for floors and beams.
It is a landscape of hills and domes with sometimes
the squares and wedges of the old federal architecture.
The Cathedral, set on a hill near the center of the city,
can be seen across miles of sunlit woodland, cane fields,
corn, vineyard, and plowland under a purple-blue sky.

◆

The farmers, prizing their independence, will usually
grow for the household a good crop of durum and emmer,
barley, apples, tomatoes, and gourds, even
when wine and walnut oil yield the richest percentage.
Most will raise and slaughter their meat, and the lamb
and pepper-ham here are especially tender and choice.
The lakes are full of pickerel, lake trout and bass,
and huge blackberries, peaches, and raspberries ripen
in summer. The vale of Les Tres Riches Heures,
where the river Kokosing wanders to join the Walhonding,
is covered with vineyards divided by windbreaks and groves

50

of walnuts that flower like amorous bridesmaids in spring.
The wine of Mohican, pressed from noble Cabernet
strains hardened by subtle genetic splicing
and all the varietal whites from the ancient Rhine valley,
is sought and drunk in Europe, in China, the planets
of Proxima Centauri, and the stars of the Small Magellanic.
Amphoras are lost in the violent Lake Michigan storms.
The season's brevity, the alkaline soil of the slopes,
and the matching of strain to the land, have produced a red
that glows like fresh oak that's got hot in the autumn sun,
and a white that catches a trembling star in its chill.

◆

At harvest time the sound of the fiddle and dulcimer
rings in the winding chains of hillbilly songs,
black woodsmoke, and bright orange pumpkins. A jew's-harp
with its wild hurdy-gurdy will raise the hair on your neck,
sounding, a moment before the warm yellow fiddle
comes in, like a Mad County melody; or a banjo, late,
when the trash-fires die, will sing the sad love of a swain.
It was from Classical Rock and Jazz, however,
that Vaisya commercial music began, not from 'Grass.
Lovers in Mansfield's willow-world district can hear
over coffee and Floridy oranges in their pretty white suites
the sound of a lonely glass trumpet, Sunday morning,
where the boy has opened the bar-room door to sweep
out the peanut shells, dust, ash, and odorous candlewax.
Jazz nearly died when brass became too expensive,
but acoustic silicon glass, with its smoothness of tone,
its anodized golden or white-metal finish, its sweetness
way up in the higher registers, growliness
down in the bass, was more than an adequate substitute.
The high musics of Brahmins and Kshatriyas came
from the astonishing twenty-first-century breakthrough that created
a new tonality reconciling the Indian, Chinese,
and Balinese scales with the great tradition of Europe.
It was science that healed the damage that science had done
loosing atonal chaos over the world:
from a study of whale music and antiphonal birdsong,
acoustic science discovered natural tonality

51

and showed how a single system could be created
which, like the Holy Way of the Garden, gave niches
to all the sweet sounds of the world; and beauty once more
was sought as the source and the end and the meaning of art.
And High Countian music was rooted in local
traditional melodies, personal tonality, ritual.

♦

The highest and saddest Mohican art of them all
is the art of war. In the late twentieth century
the heavy machines of battle began to become
so expensive that wars collapsed for lack of munitions
before either side could achieve a conceivable aim.
The weapons of horror—gas, chemical, nuclear,
biological—were practically useless, and beyond an exchange
or two, which proved to the advantage of all interested
parties except the combatants, were never used.
It was the cheap, home-grown microprocessor
that revolutionized warfare, and made it come to express
the implacable forces of human esthetic choice.
A crude homing rocket tipped with a brain
as ingenious as any veteran, but fearless and pitiless,
could frag billions of dollars of complex machinery.
The infantryman with a quiver of rockets and a laser
was the equal of several tanks or whirlybird gunships.
And then came the age of light resinite armor;
a man could withstand a hail of machine gun bullets
and even several seconds of coherent light.
And two more developments followed: the exhaustion
of Terran metallic ores, and the electronic deadlock.
Any weapon of metal greater than a blade
is not cost effective; and in the region of radar
and radio waves defensive measures frustrate
cheaply and subtly any conceivable gain
in control or intelligence offered by electronic telemetry.
So, as of old, warriors mounted and armored
in glittering plate ride forth with magical weapons
with which they speak as to friends or sing the beatsong
to carry the rhythm whose quarter tones, sixty-fourth
notes, and harmonics coordinate weapon and hero.

The great historical law of beauty is vindicated:
each age chooses its material vesture
and condition down to the tiniest detail. Just so
the image of war desired by the dream of the twentieth
century cohered into the towering mushroom cloud
according to their most beautiful theory of cause,
which attributed magical power to the parts of the whole
and its past, and predicted the end of the world by the loss
of radiant energy: the explosion that effaces distinctions,
reduces all wholes to their parts, and resolves the complexities
embroidered in matter into a burst of radiant energy,
satisfied all their nightmare lust for cleanliness,
confined as they were to the heavy oppression of one
planet, and their thick, polluting responsibility
to all future generations of Homo sapiens.
But we know that all such notions are childish:
that there's no escape into innocence back down the ladder
of being; that no reduction can tell us what
we should be; that we cannot fall back on the comfort of despair
but are bound to build the world in the human image,
and cleanse ourselves only with fluids of past pollutions.
And therefore our Knighthood's both comic and tragical, war
is imaged in armed individual men and women
playing a fatal game in the forest and field.

◆

Ruth was more and more curious about the meaning
of battle, and studied the recent history of war.
She found, alarmed, that the Black Counties had crushed
in Vaniah, Diana, and Tucky several Free
Counties, and slaughtered those who would not convert.
That summer the rumor of war was persistent;
Wyandot County was busy fending off raids
from the West, and black-sailed shipping was seen
off the northern coast of Ahiah; later that month
a Sanduskian freighter was looted and sunk, and spies
brought back the grim story of the Vanian Confederacy.
In June a small force was detached to help Tuscarawas,
and in August almost two thousand troops, half
the Mohican army, and the militia, were partially mobilized.

Ruth, who was trained in arms, wanted to go;
but Shaker, seeing her talent for leadership, kept her
at home for a greater purpose. Her best friend,
Antony Manse, went off to the wars with a song
on his fine dark lips, and so did her brother Simon.
After the wet weather of late September
there was a clearing, a frost, and suddenly all
the leaves burst into feverish negative, flame
dresses under the indigo sky; and now
the bad news started coming in.
The southern thrust had been held, it seemed, at the river,
but the north had collapsed and, in a surprise, the crossings
at Wheeling were forced by Alleganian troops ferried over
by transports at night. Many were slain, and the rest
had retreated up the long valley westward.
The rearguard had held them near the town of St. Clair
and a counterattack, two days later,
had driven the enemy back to the village of Blaine.
A truce had been called, for the rout in the North had been halted
along the line of the One Leg River and the Lakes,
but much of Tuscarawas lay in the hands of the Jihad.
Already there were stories of burnings in Salem and Wellsville,
but most of the folk had escaped, and the capital, New
Philadelphia, was saved. Everyone knew that the respite
was brief, and the County looked for some warlord to lead them
like the old banished warrior George Quincy.

◆

Later that fall the Mohican army rode in.
It was said that at times they had fought terrible odds
and that great deeds were done in the valleys about the Ahiah.
Ruth went out to greet the soldiers' return
with her friends, and a basket of roses, as was the custom.
On they came, down Gambier Street, the fife
skirling above the thump of the drum. The leaders
appeared in the long avenue of golden trees
under the brilliant scarlet dogwood berries;
first, the generals, in civil dress, cloaked
and on foot to show their submission to the people:
Moira Gioia, "Galloping Jack" Sherman,

Camilla McCloud, from another branch of the family,
who flew with the sunplane squadrons against the north.
Next behind them rode in full armor the heroes
who'd held the foe at St. Clair: among them two men
that Ruth knew well, with their white breastplates glittering,
their casques thrown back from their faces, their weapons polished.
"Which one is that?" asked Ruth's friend, "the black one who carries
himself so well, and who sings, I think, under
his breath, and looks this way and that?" "Antony
Manse is his name, but you mustn't make eyes at him."
"Who is that other, then—the tall pale one
with the two spots of red on his cheeks, whose mouth
seems ugly, though he's a fine man indeed; look
at how black his hair is, and his eyes! He frightens me, Ruth."
"That is Simon my brother, but I don't know him well,
because Faith my grandmother raised him since he was young.
You can have him if you like, but there's something bitter about him."
"And which one is that, the one that rides behind,
with the golden hair and beautiful face? You'd think
his mother's milk were scarcely out of him. What strange
blue eyes he has! And why is he wearing no armor?"
"It seems that I know him, Cressie, but I can't tell you
his name. Surely I've never seen him before—
he's not from Mohican County—but it seems as if
I'd seen him once in a dream. What an odd fellow.
Perhaps he's some sort of beggar they picked up on the road
as a mascot. Or else he'd have armor. I wonder. . . . " But now
Antony Manse has seen her at last, and turns
his horse with a flourish, and bows to her; she returns it;
he gathers her up in his arm and sets her before him
and the two of them ride on into the city.
Behind them, unarmored, James George Quincy
whom the soldiers named Rollo at the battle of St. Clair, looks on
as Antony greets that pale beautiful woman
whose hair like a cloud of fire haloes her face
and wonders why she seems to him so familiar
yet strange, as if he'd seen her once in a dream;
and beside those lovers, Simon rides in silence,
glancing at Ruth with a flush and a darkening brow.

III

◆◆◆◆◆◆◆◆◆◆◆◆◆◆◆◆◆◆◆◆◆

THE THREE
SUITORS

1. The Battle of St. Clair

"The Wheeling beachhead had been forced when we,
riding out of the morning, came at last,
too late, and saw the Tuscarawan army
falling away and leaving all their dead.
Our horses and ourselves were wearied out
and so we rested in the hills that day
and in the evening rode through valleys dark
and gorges silent, in the hope that we
might fall upon the enemy when he
should hold our friends in some last hopeless stand."
Picture the banquet hall in Old Mount Verdant,
the seiges of the long oak tables filled
with chivalry, their gorgets glittering,
their eyes, ladies and gentlemen of war,
burning with memory and candle flame.
Survivors of the Errant Company
have been commanded by Elizabeth
the Praetor, that they tell the story of
the battle of St. Clair; Simon refused,
and so did Antony, and thus it fell
upon the stranger Rollo that he speak
before the company and tell the tale.

♦

"High are those hills and deep are the ravines;
the Tuscarawans ride in fear and pain.
Surprising a Mad Countian patrol
that night, we learned the men of Somerset,
whose friends we had cut up across the river,
had grudges at their Allegany allies,
suspecting that the Alleganians
would, when the war was over, with the help
of Susquehanna and Monongahela,
partition Somerset, which they accused
of lacking Christian zeal. Our Captain, Gared
Hamilton of Tuscarawas, asked
Lieutenant Manse what profit was in this;

but Maury Edsel, who had overheard,
broke in and told a foolish fairy tale.

♦

'It seems there were three giants who were brothers—
Rioter-folk—and they had found young Jack
who was a salesman, chased him up a tree,
and waited for the morning light to show
a clear target that they might stone him down.
Jack waited patiently until they slept,
their backs against the tree; then broke a branch
and clambered down as close as he might dare,
and knocked a sleeping giant on his head.
The giant, thinking his friends had found him sleeping
and woke him up in this discourteous fashion,
fetched his brother a clip around the ear
that sent him flying. The quarrel was patched up,
and silence came; Jack did the same again.
This time a battle raged for half an hour
before domestic harmony resumed.
And so it went, until the brothers, mad
with rage, murdered each other, leaving Jack
to scramble down his tree and so escape.'

♦

And we adapted Skip's plan to our case,
and crept at night among the enemy,
and slew in silence five men from the fires
of Somerset, and ten from Allegany
and dragged the men of Somerset to where
it seemed they might have died upon a raid
against the Alleganians, and then
raised the alarm, and slipped away unseen.
After an hour's confusion, shouts of rage,
and mustering of men, we saw a column,
armed with torches, set out back to the river
whence they had come. The men of Somerset
had broken their alliance and would fight
no more against the counties of Ahiah;

among them were two rocketeer brigades.
Meanwhile, in the confusion, General
Rioja of the Tuscarawans led
his forces up the valley and away.
But in the dawn the enemy, relentless,
followed the Tuscarawans, for he knew
he had a great advantage still in force
and impetus, and knew Mohican help
was on its way to join the beaten army.
Then we decided we should sell our lives
and hold the Vanian army at the pass
and give our friends the time to get away.

◆

Riding ahead, we found a little hill
that rose within the valley, where the stream
divided and rejoined in marshy ground.
A farmer told us that the village near
the upper fork, beyond, was called St. Clair.
Here we decided we should take our stand.
A rocky outcrop, with some dogwood trees
in berry on it, gave us cover. Then
we prayed to Yahman, god of dark and death,
to Pan the god of unexhausted life,
and Sperimenh the god of human breath;
and ate our rations, and drank from the stream.
On comes the army of the Black Jihad,
their sable breastplates laced up to the chin,
their helmets closed; bright swords hang by their sides,
shields at their necks, and pennons on each lance.
The valley echoes with their battle horns.
And now we sent a herald out ahead
and called a parley, challenging the best
among their knights to fight against our best.
But as we did we heard the battering hooves
of a greathorse ridden unmercifully;
and a man in armor rode into our camp—
his black horse streaked with foam—raised up his visor,
cried that he would be one of those who rode
against the challengers, whether we would

or no. It was Simon Raven McCloud.
He'd disobeyed the order to retreat,
hearing about the stand that we would make
and came here to do battle by our side.
His wish was granted, for the enemy
being honorable, chose their finest knights
and sent them forth, armored in black and gold.
It is the custom of these Christian knights
to take the names of pagans when they fight,
turning, as they believe it, wickedness
against the wicked, as good toward the good.
Three knights there were, their helmets dark and grim:
Estramariz, Blancandrin, Valdabron.
And out to them rode our Sir Antony,
Sir Gared Hamilton, Simon McCloud.
Such was the wrath of our Ahian knights
that each one of the Vanians was unhorsed
at first encounter; two of them were slain,
the other, whom Sir Gared's lance had struck,
Blancandrin, crawled, a blinded animal.
And then came forth three other Christian Knights:
Lehelin, Gramoflanz, Florant; and they
were chevaliers of Allegany's hills.
And so the lances struck, and flexed, and split,
flinging their shining splinters in the sky,
and each knight kept his seat, and drew his sword,
and turned upon his enemy, and charged;
but Gared bled now from a shoulder wound
and Gramoflanz carried a lance point in
his thigh, and as he fought he moaned aloud.
Lehelin struck the helm of Antony;
but Antony drove with his point, and pierced
the Alleganian at his shoulder joint
and broke his heart just as he raised his hand.
And Simon, who disdained to close his visor
and called his enemy by name, and jeered,
cleft Sir Florant from neck joint to the groin,
and left that knight to clatter in the dust.
At that the army of the Vanians
roared like a tide, and swept toward our lines;

the three Ahian knights rode slowly back
and each of us prepared himself to die."

♦

"Except for me," Maury Edsel interrupted.
"I was scared shitless, which isn't a figure of speech.
I could see the blood pumping from Gared Hamilton's
armor, and feel the cold, slick, razor-sharp
metal like it was there in my gut already.
No thanks, I said, this is no place for the Skipper.
Life is like money; when you've got it, you don't worry about it,
but without it there's nothing, and that's the bottom line.
These fellows here were all out of their minds;
sure, they looked fine in their armor, singing like maniacs,
but Mrs. Edsel's little boy had one
desire, to find a hole to hide his ass.
I saw James Quincy, like an idiot, armorless,
get up and charge the Vanians, smiling all over
his face; and Mrs. Quincy rolled me over,
stood by me with a knife when they broke our line; saw Simon,
with those red spots on his cheeks, take a rest, get out
a cigar, and light up; and Captain Hamilton, with his foot
dangling off, attack the Vanian general
and cut him down, and fall with two swords in him;
and then they fell back, with only forty of us left,
and we fired our last rockets against them, and they,
thinking us greater in number, sent horsemen around
through the marshes and over the hills, and got ready to charge
from behind. I found a corpse to get under, and waited,
and heard the sound of their hooves, and peeked out and saw
James George Quincy get up with his sword
and sing out 'Aoi!' and charge the enemy horse
and I knew my species was one big awful
mistake, and closed my eyes; but our soldiers sprang up
and followed, and shouted out 'Rollo!' and then the enemy
cavalry sank in the marsh to their knees, where our warriors
could get at them; it was a smart kind of craziness after all.
I saw young Tuscarawan girls, scarce out of school,
wipe their swords clean of the blood with their hair, and sigh
as if having dried the dishes and put them away.

At last there were only seven of us left, and the rest
who would never drink wine again, make love to their lovers, or play
with their children, or settle down to a pastry or pie,
were lying among the heaps of enemy dead,
just flesh after all, with nothing to mark out the difference,
flesh of Ahiah or Vanian flesh, or mud
of the stream churned up by the hooves of the Vanian cavalry.
And what for? The right to pray to a God that we,
not somebody else, have invented? The Vanian herald
came forward, and laughed when he saw us, and asked for surrender;
I was nodding, but Simon wouldn't listen to sense.
'You cannot stand against us,' said the herald,
'and you have risked your souls against your God
enough today; the more of us you send to Heaven
the more of you are sent to Hell.' But Simon,
with his smile, drew out his sword, and struck him on the hip
so that his leg was severed, and he fell; and Simon
spoke: 'It's you, my friend, who cannot stand,
for look, your leg is off. But do not fear:
You shall have wings in Heaven, so I'm told.'
And now I knew it was all over for us,
and the Vanian troops in their fury wouldn't spare even
a harmless commercial traveler; but at that moment
as you all know, the counterattack began;
the troops from Sandusky, Mohican, and Wyandot Counties
had come in the nick of time, and we would be saved:
it was, I have to admit, a magnificent sight
to see our cavalry galloping down toward us."

◆

And if no virtue or loveliness flourishes
except it be founded in dear life itself;
if the flowers that shake into blossom over the tips
of the tree of knowledge in humanity's manifold springtimes
be nourished by roots that are humble, the humors of life;
if art is the interest we draw on the pledge of existence:
yet life, even, like money that passes from hand
to hand, takes its preciousness only from arts of commitment
and covenants we must defend with our lives, or our lives
shall be worth no more than those of the beasts of the field;

it is the airy flower that swells with desire
the great driving root, the leaf in the sun that feeds
the rings of the wood; and the wealth of wealth, the value
of value, lies in our power to count it for little.

2. An Attempted Rape

Some say that Simon had an extra chromosome;
others, that a male demon haunted and tormented him;
that he was impotent, or that he had the power
of women, to know his pleasure many times
unceasing, and that the witch his grandmother had given him that gift.
Now he is home the hero, and he sees across
the table in the waxlight glow his stepfather's favorite,
Ruth his half-sister; how her bright hair
flames about the fair and lovely oval
of her face, and the velvety pupils of her eyes spread wide
miraculously to the whites, as she stares into the dark;
and it seems he has lost his breath, and must gulp wine
till his ears roar, that the sight and smell of her not
unman him altogether. For he would in his spirit have her dead,
laid out upon her tomb, that he might love her always
and make her flesh his, whiteness and flush and freckle,
and be at home with her there in the dark forever.

◆

James and his mother ride out to the farm at Lithend,
come over the brow of the hill in the afternoon.
The valley lies, a white-gold sea of wheat
between capes and coves of red-gold autumn trees;
and the river winds there like a wreathed wake of blue.
And there they see the heavy timbered gables
and the broad roof covered with silver shingles
and the packed, iridescent, plates of solar collectors
and the great white rotor towering over
the river, and the gold domes of the silos and barns.
And Mary Quincy weeps and her son remembers

the garden where as a boy he grew delicate phloxes
and strawberries, planted an apple tree; and the place
on the bluff that he'd fashioned into a fortification;
and they both remember the grandeur and gaiety, the mad
humor of George Quincy who would never return
to his home. So they ride to the door and dismount, and strike
the glass bell by the porch; there is a cry, and old
Billy Blubaugh and Leroy Workman appear, and Marcia
Layman, carrying milk in a pail. A boy
comes out from behind the beehives and stares at the strangers.
"I always knew you'd come back," says Billy at once,
"but where is the Master?" "He died in Hattan Riot,"
Rollo says sadly, "but in battle, and mastered not easily."
Leroy Workman, hearing this, weeps, but Billy
takes him by the shoulder and says: "What kind of hello
is this for the boy and the lady? We'll mourn him later:
isn't it manna from heaven that they have returned?"
But Marcia Layman turns pale, and whispers to Billy,
and Rollo speaks: "What is the matter, my friends?
We've come to live among you again, as you see."
"How tall you are, Master," sobs the old woman. "Just right
to be your own man on your farm and look after us all."
"What grief is in that?" "Lithend," Billy says dully,
"doesn't belong to the Quincys but to the McClouds.
Being away more than five years your claim
lapsed, so the lawyer said; Shaker McCloud took it over,
showing cause that we weren't told of and don't understand."
"Then we have lost our home," says Mary Quincy,
and gives a great sigh. "George, George," she whispers,
"Could you not think of the boy?" And James overhears her
and asks what she means; but she shakes her head, and turns
away to her horse. But James embraces his friends
and inquires of them all that has happened since he, as a child,
rode away to the east. And only reluctantly will they,
at his pleading the grief of his mother, permit him to go
and return to the city as the evening frost falls.

◆

There is some debate, to Rollo's surprise, in the Senate
as to whether he and his mother be permitted to stay;

a secret discussion in which, it is said, Shaker
McCloud takes a prominent role. But at last it's decided,
in view of the Quincys' heroic service in war,
to confirm their citizenship of the County. What,
asks James of himself, does McCloud hold against me?
But he takes up service with a weaponsmith, a twentieth share;
at night he attends courses at the university;
and Mary tutors the children of Huddibras Manse,
the elder brother of Antony and that Celia
who married Mungo McCloud five years ago.
James and Mary are cold that winter in their poor
rented room by the river; the town under snow is pretty
but feels to them not their own. But at Christmas they sit
in the warm Cathedral and hear the old carols: "Above
thy deep and dreamless sleep the silent stars
go by" and find that each has a gift for the other.

◆

Ruth gets her degree next spring, and turns
her studies to contract and property law. How,
she asks, as if it had never been asked before,
does that great mystery of mine and thine
by which the world is sacramentalized
into the flesh that clothes the human spirit
take its first root and justification? Property; proper;
propriety; propre: the word itself questions
the meaning of I and thou as merely what is contained
by the skin of the individual. What is the individual?
Is my hand mine, or me? My heart? My family?
What of the food in my belly? Am I a flash
riding the neurons moment by moment? Or the nervous
system itself? Or the body? But naked when others are clothed,
where is my dignity human? As a craftsman, my tools
are part of my body; a farmer, my lands; a scholar,
the books and the microprocessors wherein I carry
a large part of my memory. And what of my children?
They have the choice to give up, it seems to Ruth,
just so much of their heritage as they take on the work
of being themselves and not an extension of me.
And if they inherit, they choose to become their family,

the name, not the personal anecdote: the convention,
not the creature that loves, dies, is damned
or is saved. If my possessions take on from me
a tincture of private fleshly sensitiveness,
so I take on from my ownership something impersonal,
real, objective, immortal, conventional, dead.
And Ruth sees the kenosis, the frigid sacrifice
of such a vocation; to subdue the face to the mask,
to crucify flesh on the cross of the public service;
to lose the self in the good of the body politic.

◆

And so she works at the Tory party grass-roots
organization, begins to accept invitations,
finds in the sweetness of friendship with Antony Manse,
a scion of that great Claudius Manse
the Chief Justice and Senator, both virtue and necessity.
She meets her old playfellow James Quincy
sometimes at lectures or the grand social evenings
that Huddibras Manse puts on; through Mary the governess
the Manses have come to know her mysterious son,
so quiet in manner, with his threadbare cloak and hat.
But Ruth avoids him, and questions herself angrily
why; and he looks at her sometimes across
the room, and listens whenever she speaks. There
is another visitor sometimes, her dark half-
brother Simon; and one evening, two summers after
the truce of St. Clair, he offers to drive her home.

◆

She accepts, but is unaccountably shaky about it;
she says goodbye to Antony, but leaves her shawl,
a delicate wisp of violet mohair, over
the arm of a chair. Simon's wagon is drawn
by one of Faith Raven's ebony horses:
they set out the ten miles to Wolverton Hill.
It has been one of those afternoons of Ahiah
that make us remember how far out at land we live
in the continent's violent climates. A haze lay over
the hills, and the light was yellowish-green, and the sun

boiled like a pink bulb of molten glass:
now a fleet of vague clouds has closed in
so tall that their creeping, pearly-white topsails collide
at the zenith, but still the sun shines on from below
and all the lush cushions of creeper and vine have a glow
of viridian green like the beetle's coppery vesture,
and the thunder sounds as if it were hours ago.
The storm catches them halfway home: a rush
of shivery wind, a stillness, and seven great drops
of rain in the road, that steam infernally. Over
the hills there marches a wall of water, a haze
of mist blows through the vertical rain. And now
there's a rattle, as if the earth's wheels had flung up a scatter
of stones: hail, which in a flash has whitened
the hedges and covered the road. Simon controls
the horse and drives for a barn that looms in the gathering
dark. Inside they get down and stand in the beast-smell
barely out of the vapor that floats through the doorway.
Simon's hair has covered a cheek with black paint;
Ruth's pink frock is plastered against
her chest and her naked bosom. She picks at the fabric
and laughs, her red hair darkened to purple, her skin
flushed and cooled with the white and distilled waterdrops.
Simon looks upon her with what feels like resentment
or terror, only slowly recognized as desire.
There is a clean crack, like the split of an arc,
and where they are looking a fireball, bright as a nerve,
but mild pink, sits in the air and goes out.
Both of them feel in their fingers and feet a wave
of needles and pins: Simon has moved behind her,
and has sheltered her head with his arm, and has placed his other hand
flat on her navel, and smells the milky smell of her
all afternoon cooped up, girl-flesh, clothes
damp and wrinkled at creases and pleats. She moves
away, and looks at his face, and at once she could die
with the terror, his ugly mouth, the spots of pink
on his cheek, the rage of terrible justice, the grief.
He has touched with himself her buttock through the cloth
and fate has determined the whole thing must be done.
He moves on her, pleading; she catches herself, is bright,

prosaic; and shuddering, chatters away to distract him;
he with his dreadful strength rips the dress
from her shoulders and bares the bird-wing clavicle,
the flutter of plexus, the two pits of the hips:
she does not know it, but cruellest of all, the egg
in her loin, dispatched by the terrified organ's forlorn
and immortal spasm, like the rich cluster of berries
that burst out on the tree that is stricken, comes down
as she fumbles with Kshatriya courage for the knife at her thigh.
The blow grazes his ribs but he twists the blade
from her hand, and the blood trickles over her ribcage
and knee-tendon, ankle, and instep. He holds the knife
to her throat, but she, with a jerk, tries to impale
herself on it: he flings it away. But hooves, hooves!
It is Antony Manse, he has leapt from his horse, in his arm
the shawl she left at the house and that he is returning.
He seizes Simon by the throat, and throws him aside;
with a little moan of grief and pity he drapes
the shawl over the flesh of his sweetheart, and turns
to murder his enemy. But Simon has clasped his hands
together into a club, and smashed them down
on the black wooly head of his rival, who drops like a stone.
With a curse Simon leaps upon Antony's horse
and rides away in the gathering night. The sky
has swept clear and is blue, but a great shoal of feathery
cirrus blazes with blood from the sunken sun.

◆

Simon is caught at the house of his grandmother Faith
in the valley of Avalon. He does not resist his capture
but speaks no word of repentance, will not drop his eyes.
At the trial he makes no defense and refuses to speak:
Shaker McCloud, his legal father, presses
for death, but Ruth, who is pale and grave but otherwise
completely composed, asks that his punishment be
to work for a term of years as a nurse in a hospital
tending the ugly sick. The judge and jury
concur with this penalty: Simon is asked whether
he will or will not endure it, or whether with honor
he will take his own life and expunge his crime in a moment.

But still he says not a word; and the judge has no choice
but to declare him an outlaw, strip off his clothes,
turn his possessions over to his kin, and send
him forth to fend for himself as a dangerous animal.
By law he has two days' grace; he goes first
to his grandmother's; she gives him clothes and a horse; he flees
eastward, and Shaker unleashes his hounds, and pursues.
Among his companions are Antony Manse, and James.
They track him over the border to Tuscarawas,
and with the permission of the local officials, all
the way to the new truce line, where they lose him.
But Simon finds his way to the council of Elders
that governs religious observance in the Black Counties:
and soon he begins to pour poison into their ears.

◆

Ruth is unharmed: her passionate rational wit
and courage sustain her: but a stain of evil hangs
in the air; everyone notices ears of corn
whose whorls of grain are deformed, and a five-legged lamb
is brought to the fair by a trader. Later that summer
Celia Manse McCloud falls sick—a disturbance
affecting the ovaries, thyroid, lymph, and pituitary,
and a craving for certain unclean kinds of foods;
as a result she cannot feed her new baby.
The doctors are unable to make a coherent diagnosis:
the chief pathologist, Master Mercurius, turns
the case over to Catherine McCloud, who is now a well-known
diviner and reader of dreams. Despite the fact
they are sisters-in-law, Doctor Mercurius believes
that the art of Catherine McCloud will pierce through the veil
of immediate relations, lay open the source of affliction.
And so it proves; the basket of cornhusks and thimbles
and rags from the Manse-McCloud house is shaken, and spilled
on the table before the diviner: she sees at once
the long spiked tendrils and fingers of evil
darting among the branches of the family tree,
forking at crotches, and cankering flower and fruit.
She speaks: "The rage of Simon the outlaw has taken
its dwelling in Ruth Jefferson McCloud, and has passed

through her to the body of Celia Manse. Ruth
must make sacrifice swiftly, and so the pollution will pass,
the defilement be purged away. It is unjust
that the woman should pay for the evil spawned by the man:
but so Pan has ordained the world's economy;
justice less beautiful, though lovely indeed, than being."
At that she yawns and her voice returns to its wonted
habit and pattern of speech: "That, my dears,
is the ghosts' theory; and Daddy, don't look so grim."

◆

Every event in the world sends out a series
of shells of waves whose structure preserves with perfect
fidelity the shape of its cause and original. No
part of the universe, small though it be, is cut off
from anywhere else, but is knowable everywhere, given
sufficient powers of detection and inference. Those
powers are present in the cortex of Homo sapiens
which exceeds in its information capacity the cube
of the number of physical particles known to exist.
A God would be dizzied by so much trivial knowledge
and soon would devise a way of ignoring the bellow
and bawl of the world. Which indeed we did, being gods,
but found, once our vision had cleared, that which robs us of godhead:
the blessed presence of other persons, other
minds, which second-guess us at the same moment
that we second-guess them. We are twice removed
from divine omniscience, once by the need to act,
and once by the happy tragedy of sharing awareness
with others. But that ancient, primitive, goddy power
remains, and diviners, become as a little child,
may seize it and know once more the ordinary gnosis:
it is the ignorance lovers and heroes and poets
possess that is truly extraordinary, that rises above
the infinite wisdom of beasts, infants, and gods.
But healing will often require that we retrace the path
by which we arrived at complete humanity: and so
Ruth McCloud obeys her sister the seer
and stands at the altar under the many-colored
dome of Pan, dressed in a single white garment

of silk, a white ewe tethered before her.
The braziers burn; the knife without a handle
that Ruth holds by the tang, strokes over
the throat of the docile animal, and sheds its blood
so her wrist is hot with the sweet innocent jet of it;
the wooly beast drops, and kicks with a twitch, and is still;
the knife does its work; the meat is cast into the fire;
wine, honey, and milk are poured on the flames;
the beautiful stone of the floor is washed with clear water;
the prayers are said, and the celebrant passes the blade
to the other participants, among them James and Antony;
the knife at last is also thrown in the fire,
its metal, reforged and purified, to be hammered again
into an instrument hallowed and polished for sacrifice.
And at that moment Ruth suddenly finds
that the dull headache she had not known that she had
has passed away and she is as free of it now
as before Simon had placed his hand on her belly.
And from that day Celia loses the ashen
cast to her skin, which blooms once more in its own
beautiful teakwood sheen, and the baby sucks
at her breast hungrily, gasps, and ceases to cry.

3. Antony and James

James George Quincy had grown into a man
tall and straight and beautiful; his fair hair
fell in curls along his slender jaw;
his eyes, that seemed blind, they were of a blue so pale,
burned with more than a hero's trouble, and saw
much that he never spoke. His work with the hammer
had broadened his shoulders; his learning had taught him questions,
reverence, criticism. In that first moment of anguished
bewilderment, seeing the girl on Gambier Street
who rode off with Antony Manse, he had not known how
to content his soul: it was as if his heart
had been scalded with honey, his breath broken on a wheel;

the pale cheeks and the eyes as hot as her hair
rose like a dawn in him. At first, poor fool, he knew not
what he felt, though it seemed like something he knew as a child,
like Christmas perhaps, the ache of the stored gifts,
waking to Christmas-tree smells, the rustle of paper;
or earlier, how it felt to be lifted and fed, or falling
asleep in your own comfortable bed. Later
he knew it as love, seeing her lit by the candles
at the feast of triumph afterwards; and then, at the College,
he saw the respect they held her in, heard her debate
her professors, and fell into a mute despair:
how might he, a brute and a stranger, deserve
at her hands that she know of his love? He came
to the Manses' soirees, and watched her in silence;
and on that very evening of the storm, had thought
to offer his own worn buckboard for the ride;
indeed, was approaching when Simon showed her to the door.
Her eyes met his, however, with a puzzled
glance; and in her confusion she forgot her shawl.
James, again, would have gone after her with it,
but Antony saw the direction of his troubled stare,
plucked up the violet thing, and told the company he
would carry it to her. After the trial and the hunt
(at neither of which James was made to feel welcome)
he dreamed a dream, wherein Simon had stolen the ring
that Mary, the mother of James, had always worn:
and they hunted the thief with dogs, and found him at last
in the caverns of Hattan Riot: but Simon turned on them
and lo! to his terror and nausea Simon's face
was the face of James himself. And waking he felt
with a pang like death a longing to get back his farm,
Lithend, and be master there as his father had been.
Next day he attended the sacrifice; suddenly
all was changed for him then, and he knew, seeing
her naked arm with the knife, that Ruth was his friend
for all of his life, and that he would make her his wife.

◆

But in his studies he has learned much that weighs on him:
for in taking the role of hero and lover he travails

a path churned by history, trod by the feet
of so many: every action's subtended by tedious
ghosts in the night, by ridicule during the day:
he has a friend at the College called John-Paul Snipes
whose nickname for James is The Sorrows of Young Werther.
He fears he is not Prince Hamlet, nor was meant to be;
and no more like him than he is to Hercules.
For every hero has spent something left over
by a predecessor, whether by theft or parody, lies
or calculated humility; Achilles more tragic
than Gilgamesh mourning his friend, and more hysterical;
Odysseus making a virtue of second best,
always the family man; Parsifal owing
it all to the Grail, with his Christ-face covering
over all the contingencies, all human vanities;
and the anti-heroes, making a vice of necessity.
And every lover claimed that the world had not dawned
till then on a love like his own; till they solved the problem
four hundred years ago, sending the young and the hot
into bed with each other with hygienic parental blessings,
allowing no time for the pernicious organic disease
called love to darken the mixture. And even that
didn't work; Platonic idealism reared its ugly
head, and the young refused their elders' potato-love.
What's left that is pure? For James, to take the path
though late and far behind, and follow it faithfully
through to the end: that's his originality.
And perhaps there is no before and after in this
race, for the road of history's only the starting line,
the new evolution at ninety degrees to the old;
the palm at the end of the spirit remains to be won.

◆

But Ruth has no conception of James' distress;
the strangeness about him she felt at first is explained
by their acquaintance as children. Though the strangeness oddly remains,
she gives little thought to it, finds him a dull young man
whose politeness mitigates somewhat his only bad habit
of hanging about when there's no reason to do so.
And all her thoughts are bent toward Antony Manse,

the debonair prince of his line, her friend and colleague,
fellow leader in local party affairs,
and excellent capable lover, as she finds one night
at the Trois Clefs Hotel in Mansfield, after
an evening of jazz, champagne, incognito, and dancing.
For having fully explored their compatibilities
these young intelligent folk have decided to take
the test for marriage qualifications, will seek
the consent of Shaker McCloud and Claudius Manse
as soon as she has completed her second degree
and he is commissioned a Major in the Mohican army.

◆

And so when James finds her walking alone one fall
morning on Middle Path between classes and joins her
she scarcely attends him at first. But something has changed
in his tone, and surprised, she listens more closely. He speaks
of their games as children, how they had invented a way
by merely closing their eyes, to travel wherever
they wished, using the power of thought: to distant
worlds, or the past, or the future; how only they
had the gift; when they flew, each knew that the other
was flying beside him; how good it was to return.
And the note in his voice, of calling them both to the real
world both of them knew but denied, its shakiness
nevertheless, reminds her of something horrible
she has forgotten: Simon's attempt at rape,
and through that, the moment when she was a girl, and Simon
was sent to his grandmother Faith's, and James went away
into another country, and Shaker made her
his favorite. She shivers, and moves a little away;
but now James catches her eye, and she sees
with a shock in her breath, how foolishly she
has ignored this youth: how there is something archaic
yet infinitely refined in his concentration, his singleness:
like the ginkgo leaves that they walk through, flat gold
with flanges and flutes, scalloped into a shape so simple
that its elegance tastes of the brutal; and yet its design
from the dawn age of the trees, the Chinese
silver apricot, the ancient link of the orders

gymnosperm, angiosperm—male trees grown
for their beauty, silver-boled—suggests the civilized
violence of cultivation that exceeds the forces of nature.
Her study of leaves is a fugue of the mind from the fear of her
terrifyingly patient companion. "Why do you follow me?"
now she breaks out. "You are noble, I know, and would not
hurt me nor wish me harm; but we are no longer
children, and I am engaged to be married, and you
seem to come from a time where I live no more."
"Lady, if you catch, as you do, my intention, then whether
you wish it or no, you live in the same world as I."
"But I have in very deed visited those stars
that we traveled in fancy. It's all, you see, in the real
past for me." "I don't ask return to the past.
But this moment is the past for some present
which will redeem it, if you are willing." "James
Quincy, I shall not take the risk. I owe
too much, and indeed my happiness lies with my duty.
Goodbye." But he holds her eye for a moment, and now
there is more intimacy between them than she
has ever known with another; she shakes with grief
and anxiety, mingled strangely with exaltation;
but turns away, and her grey coat rustles
the golden ginkgo leaves like the wind of the fall.

♦

The races of man, we know, owe their beautiful
differences largely to the choices of generations.
The sweet fold of the eye, the skin's burnish,
the carven fullness of lip, the curl of the hair,
stature or grace or swiftness, elongation
of finger or thigh, even the depth or subtlety,
noble simplicity, style or humor or brilliant
sensuality, sharpness or might of the mind
were chosen, in chant and ritual, tribe after tribe,
according to patterns laid down by the art of the culture,
as a people's music alters the rhythm of footfall,
painting alters the tilt of a cheekbone, the line
of a tress or an eye. For what was most beautiful caught
the heart of a lover, and love passed that trait

invisibly on to the fat and beloved baby
pinching the breast whose ripeness dizzied his father.
We are the holy and dangerous beast that dared
to domesticate not only our plant and animal servants,
but also ourselves: and not for usefulness only
but chiefly for beauty, the blazon of expressed shapeliness.
And so the heroic hang of the Great Dane,
the pretty baroque of the King Charles Spaniel,
the deathlike elegance of the Siamese cat, the fire
of the fighting-fish, bulbous flash of the poi, pout
and delicate feather of pigeon and dove that Darwin
admired, crimson petals of rose and peony,
are only attendants on the sovereign differences given
to this clan of mutated monkeys, to itself by itself.
Once a marriage between a white and a negro
was looked on with horror, for men believed that the races
differed by nature, not, as we now know,
by the choice of persons following, altering what
the cultural rules of beauty dictated. But we
especially prize the unique, and therefore are pleased
when lovers break the habit of choosing a beauty
that resembles that of themselves and their family:
and so the announcement by Ruth and Antony that they
intend to take the required tests for marriage
seems to Mount Verdant society the happiest outcome.
It is our custom also that parents and relatives
should share in the work of consent, and thus help
to make the projected marriage a real one: for marriage
is real so far as it penetrates into the world
of interpersonal verification and gains
the consent of its living environment. Lovers, of course,
as lovers, live in a world of their own, a dream
that need not ever encounter the touch of reality;
and therefore we reverence them, treating them lovingly
just as we honor the harmless insane. Marriage,
though, is the work of a lifetime, the greatest of arts.
And therefore the kin of the bride and the groom must set
them tests of their own and be satisfied; Shaker McCloud
and Hilda, Antony's mother, are deputed by family
councils to act for the kin-groups and set up the tests.

With six months of training Ruth and Antony
pass the County examinations and are ready
to try the family tests. James is unmoved:
he knows that the marriage shall not take place, and lays
his plans. From time to time he sees Ruth
and his mood is kindly, as one might be in a game
one's opponent has lost, should the loser refuse to concede
but struggle in vain against the grip of the victor.
Even when Ruth completes to perfection the tasks
enjoined by the Manse family council, James
keeps his composure, but awaits the testing of Antony.

4. The Three Tests

The first two ordeals follow traditional models,
but Shaker, who's biased in favor of Antony, gives
the suitor a start by matching the tasks to his talents.
The first labor's to hunt and capture that beast
known as the Vampire Boar of Spring Mountain,
as a proof of command over the world of things.
The Vampire Boar was the fruit of genetic experiments
that sought to produce a swine of great size that would live
on a liquid diet, devoting to body-weight all
the metabolic energy normally given digestion
and evacuation. Genes were spliced in from the wild
stock; something went wrong; the brute was savage,
intelligent, tusked and gigantic; a carnivore needing,
because of its crude digestive canal, to feed
off the choicest of liquid nutrients, blood: addicted
to blood. Several beasts escaped from their farm
in Tuscarawas during a raid, went feral,
bred, and took refuge from hunters up in the hills
north of Walhonding River. The Vampire Boar
of Spring Mountain dwelt in a region of caves
with its mother, and raided the farms, murdering cattle

and sheep, and now had recently taken a man
who'd been found, his throat and chest torn open by terrible
strokes of his tushes, and bloodless white as a sheet.
Antony must, with only a bladed weapon,
destroy this enemy to the bosom of Man; without
beaters or firearms, with boar-hounds only, and spear.
The second ordeal tests mastery over the flesh:
he must walk, without falling, a rope over the torrent
of Avalon that crashes down through its gorge from the lake.
But Shaker believes that his suitor has the measure
of both these tasks, for Antony's hounds and hunting
are famous, and he is an athlete and acrobat, trained
in feats of balance and fine bodily control.
But one more test remains, not chosen
by Shaker, but, oddly, by Ruth's grandmother Faith
who insists at this moment on seeing her rights in the child
and adding a third ordeal for Antony Manse.
It is a strange test, but ruled legitimate:
Wolverton Hill has many hives for the bees
that feed off the sweetness and seed the apple blooms carry,
and one of the hives is sick and endangers the others.
To know the disease you must count the number of bees
that die, over a span of seventy-two hours,
and note the times in the cycle of day and night
of the greatest and least hours and periods of affliction.
It's this unforbidding but tedious task that the suitor's
enjoined to perform: it is a test of command
not over the world or the flesh, but the spirit.

◆

Two days before Antony takes the first test
James visits Wolverton Hill Farm.
It's early spring, and he rides through Avalon Valley
as if through a world of snow: the boughs of blossom,
pear, cherry, and apple, burden the cool
spring air with buttery sweetness; the leaves
are not out, but the buds veil the woodlanded hillsides
with mists of delicate green: the forest floor,
for the only time of the year, is beaten with festive
sunshine, and daffodils, crocuses, aconite carpet

the mold. It's the first time since he was a boy
that James has been in these woods. Memory often
leaves but a sketch, and return to the memorized place
completes, fills out, colors the picture more richly
and sets a varnish over the freshness of first impression;
but this spring world is itself scarcely
more than a scene designer's sketch on a backdrop:
a charcoal zigzag of branches, a highlight here,
a powdery spray of light green, a wash of blue,
and great masses of white and pink flung on
by a brush as full as a mop. Memory now
is a brown and polished affair compared with the violent
spring of this continental valley, blown
by the sunlight into a burst of tentative forms
and colors of spilt milk, baby toys, snow,
cream, blushes, pollen, green powder-paint.
And he rides to the black gingerbread house of Faith
Raven under the hill, and asks the way
(for he has forgotten) and a cup of water please;
and then he spurs up the winding path
through larches and silver birch groves and small rowans
till the way breaks out on the hilltop and there before him
is the noble rambling many-eaved house of McCloud.
And as he approaches, the giant Shaker McCloud
comes out on the porch, his hair as white as the snow,
and servants run up with cudgels and halberds, and stand
ready on either side. "Welcome, stranger,
to Wolverton Hill, if indeed," says Shaker, "you are
a stranger to this place." "I am no stranger, but come
in friendship that I might teach my hosts to see me
not as a friend only, but as one of their own.
My name is James George Quincy, and my father
was George Quincy of Lithend, and my mother was Mary
Madison from Loudonville in the North. I fought
at Triadelphia and was one of the seven that lived
after the battle of St. Clair. I bear the sword
called Adamant, and I am the last heir of the Quincys."
"That name is no friend to me," says Shaker.
"What do you will of us here, that we may swiftly
grant your desire, if it is one we have power

and inclination to grant? We would not keep you longer
than needful, from taking your way hence to what
business you may have elsewhere." "I thank you, Sir,
for your courtesy. But my chief business lies here. I have come
to ask for the hand of Ruth your daughter in marriage."
"Do you not know she is engaged to another?"
"I know this, and ask only that, should he not meet
the tests, I might, with your daughter's agreement, be permitted
to try them myself." Shaker McCloud is puzzled
by this young man, but it seems to him that he sees,
now, the reason for this request. "You speak,"
he says, "as one who has other purposes than that
you propose. Let us be straight with each other. I,
as I said before, have no love for your family.
You, no doubt, wish to recover the land
that your father possessed and that I, with good reason, was granted.
You did not need to come to me thus, sideways,
to make my daughter a means of pursuing your grievance."
"You do me ill," says James, "thus to interpret
my speech. It's your daughter I come for, not for my lands.
If I came on that theme you should know it clearly enough."
"You make me angry, boy, to continue dissembling.
Therefore I make your honor the price of your lands.
The land itself I hold of little account:
the unhappy purpose I kept it for, now has dissolved,
and you may have it at once upon one condition:
that you give up your claim to my daughter and drop your pretense.
Indeed, you buy dearly what would have cost you nothing:
for I would have given the land had you but asked,
but now I say that you have my permission to woo
my daughter, but only if then you renounce your claim
to your lands. Fool! for she would never accept you,
and you, without hounds or the skill of the rope, would never
pass the ordeals. Take your lands and depart
without honor. Even your father knew his disgrace
and made his exile a kind of redemption. Speak!"
"Old man, you are the fool, not I.
For I here renounce my lands, and accept your permission
to win your daughter if I am able. You
shall be my father, and I your son, whether

you will or no; but I accept nothing but this
at your hands: the hand of your daughter in marriage. Farewell!"
So saying, he turns his horse, and rides from the courtyard;
and the old man, despite his wrath, knows
that his daughter has conquered something her father could not.

◆

When Ruth hears of this meeting, a fear and a joy
so strange contend in her, she scarcely knows what she does:
but takes her pen in her hand, and writes a poem
to James, and a brief note to her father. To James:
"What love could not win, the love of honor has won.
You have my consent, if Antony fail, and if you
have the luck to succeed in the test, to take my body
and soul in exchange for yours: for though you shall fail
it would become me ill to deny you that
which costs me nothing, when you were willing to give
your birthright away for the chance to give me yourself."
And then to her father: "If Antony fail, James
George Quincy has my permission to take
the test, and if he succeed, he shall have me. Ruth."

◆

But Antony leaves with his hounds and his spear, and she
sees the sun shine on his metal, remembers his sweetness
as lover and friend; and she weeps as he rides away
with his esquire down Gambier Street into the east.
A week passes; and now a different cavalcade
returns from the hunt: the squire leading the horse
of Antony, on which he is bound and scarcely stays upright:
his face ashen, and a white bandage about
his upper thigh. Behind, the squire's horse
drags a makeshift frame on which can be seen
the huge bloody head of a vampire boar,
its tushes yellowed with foam, and flies on its wounds.
The dogs are fewer now, two of them limping,
their flappy mouths panting, whine in their noses.
Antony's passed the first test, at a cost. Having tracked
the brute to its lair, and held it at bay, he withstood
its charge and pierced it from breast to gut with his spear;

83

but as he dragged it away, its mother, a beast
larger still, enraged by the death of her mate and offspring,
her coarse-lidded eye red with rage and malice,
burst from the brush and gored the man in the groin.
The esquire drove the mother away with arrows
and laid the marvelous salves of Mohican medicine
over the wound. Refusing other means,
Antony asked for his horse, that he might return
mounted and undefeated to Ruth his mistress.

◆

The wound heals swiftly, and after three weeks
Antony asks to be shown the second ordeal.
Out of the lake at Avalon winds a fair stream
that comes to a reef of hard red sandstone
and cuts through in a series of gorges and falls.
At its narrowest point the gorge is thirty feet wide,
and Shaker's servants lead the suitor thither
and give him a braided rope forty feet long
and show him two trees where he can make it fast.
Tying one end, he makes a noose of the other,
casts it across until it catches a branch,
climbs down the cliff, fords the rock-choked torrent,
catches the rope and belays it, making sure it is tight.
The whole place is blurred with the sound of the falls
that seems to grow and fall in the ear's fantasy
like surf or the gale in the trees. Antony mounts
the rope, sways in a crouch for a moment, stands
erect, and starts the perilous passage. Halfway
across, a puff of the breeze unbalances him;
he stoops, recovers, completes the crossing at a run.

◆

There remains only the last test, the test
of the hive, that the suitor stave off for three days
that little death called sleep, and so lay claim
to the deathlessness of generation; count the deaths of the bees
and so give life to the swarm; share in the work
that distills the humble gold and the white milk
of the wick for the sweet and the light of the household. Antony

84

holds it a light task indeed; but by the sixtieth
hour he knows that it is the hardest. We
are so made that attention, the very flame of our life,
blows out in a moment. And in the sixty-fourth hour
his head drops on his breast, and he sleeps like a child.

◆

So all is changed and expectation reversed.
In his grief and shame Antony wastes and falls sick;
Like fate James presents himself for the County
marriage test, having prepared many months in secret.
But now in a different quarter events have moved,
history stretches and yawns; Douglas McCloud,
the merchant-adventurer, plays on occasion the spy
for Mohican County, and has come in with news. To the west
the great Missippian League of Free Counties
has met with defeat from the armies of the Rod of the Lord:
and there is a rumor a new Messiah has risen
in the East, and the final crusade prepares.
The five years' peace seems to be ending.
Shaker McCloud is called to the Senate, and Ruth
decides to run for the office of local elector
on the Tory platform of economic deflation,
and the improvement of military quality over quantity.
James is offered a new commission as Captain
in recognition of services done at St. Clair.

◆

No one believes that James, though he has passed
the County examinations for marriage, will succeed
in the family tests where Antony failed. He is jeered
when he sets forth without boar-hounds or even a spear
to bring in the Vampire Boar's mother. On his buckboard
he carries a cage, for he has sworn to capture
the brute alive, an oath which arouses much merriment.
His only weapon's a knife; beside the wagon
trots his old friend McArgus, half beagle
and half retriever, with a black spot on his face
and one on his back, and a wise look in his eye.
Ruth cannot bear to watch him depart and witness

the laughter of the crowd: he looks for her there, but not
finding her, joins in the mirth of the others, offering
pigs' feet for sale, cheap if they pay in advance.
But when he has left the city he weeps for an hour.
After a day's journey he reaches the hills
where the great beast is reported to roam, and lodges
in the lonely house of a farmer whose crops have been ruined.
In the morning McArgus picks up the scent of the boar
in the gullied hillsides over the Walhonding River.
The leaves have begun to come out and the grass is choked
with violets. McArgus, who takes his time, pisses
with professional care against an oak, and resumes
his work. James follows. At noon they reach
the odd region of hummocks and dusty shrubs
beaten by winding tracks where the boar has its dwelling:
it's a region once mined for its coal, and oddly valleyed
and ridged, like the antres and deserts of storybook dragons.
He finds a place where several boar tracks converge
and now he does something strange. Drawing his knife,
he strikes a wound in the heel of his left hand.
With the blood he anoints both sides of the blade;
then buries the hilt in the ground, and wedges it tight
with stones so that the blade is standing out firmly.
And now, with a whistle, he calls McArgus, who's rummaging
round in the bushes, and sets out back to the wagon.
The following day he returns with a coil of rope.
As he expects, the great boar is lying, bloated
and gasping, on the path by the knife. Seeing him there
she squeals horribly, tries to get up, and falls;
James must restrain McArgus from worrying her.
He ties a noose in the rope, drops it over
the head of the boar, and makes her get up; she tries
to charge him, collapses, becomes quite docile, allows
him to lead her back to the wagon and up a ramp
into the cage. What has happened is this:
smelling the blood on the knife, she stops on the path
from her watering hole to investigate; licks at the blade
and slices open her tongue on the razorlike edge.
But now the knife is covered with boar's blood and she,
addicted, must lick the stuff off. In minutes her tongue

is in ribbons, but now her snout and her jowls are bleeding
and the blood and the pain provoke in the brute a frenzy
of hunger, soon to be sharpened by thirst and the loss
of blood. For an hour or more she gorges on blood
and at last, her belly bursting with protein, she falls
in a faint of weakness. There James finds her
next morning, and by the time he has carried her back
to Mount Verdant, she's fully recovered and very ferocious.
This time James makes no jokes with the people
but carefully lowers the cage to the lawn of the house
the McClouds use when in town, and takes his departure.

♦

The experts are saying that James will break his neck
in Avalon Gorge, and his mother begs him not
to attempt the crossing. He is no acrobat, nor
in any one skill or knowledge can he compare
with those who have given their lives to its mastery, save
for the art of war. But in all trades and mysteries,
by marrying natural wit with what knowledge he has,
questioning earnestly, running the matter through
in his fancy, and likening that which he does not know
to that which he knows; by following always the law
of his curiosity, casting himself when he acts,
mind, passion, imagination, into
the act itself, he has become an apprentice
ready at need to take up whatever employment
the moment demands. And often his enemy finds
that this species of simpleton's hard to bring in.
James rides to the gorge; they show him the rope and the trees.
But instead of acting at once, he casts himself
down on the ground cross-legged, and stays there an hour.
At last he asks for the rope and at once begins
to pick it apart. It is a rope of seven
braided strands: he separates four from three.
When the whole rope has thus been unwound, as the weak
hydrogen bonds are broken when the spiral ladder
of genes is split in order to replicate, James
splices the ends together to fashion a rope
nearly eighty feet long, which he then casts over the chasm,

knots at the far end, runs up the tree
and knots again, and casts the end back to the bank
where he started. Crossing the stream once more
he makes fast the end, and now possesses a bridge
with a handrail, that he runs swiftly across and back.

◆

But no device will serve for the last test,
the test of endurance of death, unless that device
be one of the mind and spirit alone. James
does not delay, but after a night of sleep
settles down in the house of the bees. They have erected
an open hut, with a lamp and a table and chair
so that the bees may come and go as they will
but the observer will not suffer discomfort. Servants
will fetch him meals and whatever assistance he needs.
After a day of recording and observation
James finds his device, his trick of the spirit.
The servants notice that James is taking more notes
than his strict mandate requires: he asks for a stopwatch,
a camera, acoustic and chemical sensors, graph paper,
microscope, rulers, and pens. He covers reams
of paper with figures, notations, diagrams, sketches,
asks for a microprocessor, information
on local flora, the diurnal cycles of bees,
demands tiny resinite labels to mark
the bees, and appoints a clever lad his assistant.
In deeper and deeper excitement he follows his studies,
asks for a dictaphone, starts to dictate, but must drop
the work when new information comes in. After
seventy-two hours the servants come back
to relieve him. He waves them away impatiently, lest
they disturb an experiment; will not be interrupted;
and at last, after eighty-one hours, emerges with shouts
of delight. It turns out an anticlimax: James
has merely rediscovered the marvelous findings
of Henri Fabre and Karl von Frisch and the others
about the communal life of the bees: their dances,
division of labor, royal jelly, beebread
and cell architecture, chemical messengers, cooling

and heating the hive, the way the genetic stakes
are beautifully matched to the risks and the profits, the mind
and heart of the swarm. Somewhere among the columns
of figures he finds a precise account of the deaths
of the bees: sixty-one hundred and thirty-nine.

IV

◆◆◆◆◆◆◆◆◆◆◆◆◆◆◆◆◆◆◆◆◆

THE
GRIEF OF LOVE
AND WAR

1. The Frost-Bride

And thus to everybody's astonishment James
and Ruth are married that summer, standing before
the high altar in the apse of Sperimenh: Shaker,
whose honor will not suffer this rite to go any
the less solemnly marked than if Antony Manse
had been groom, has spared no expense of obligation
and time. The Flamen blesses this covenant: nature
here puts forth its amazing blossom of culture:
the garden springs from the sacred wood, the spring
from the mold of the fall. Here the economy takes
its root, and the household its living foundation. Palestrina
and Mozart and Bach dance in the brasses and strings
and rise to a shriek of joy in the sweet voices
of boys: it is as if a wreath of angels
skipped in a ring round the blazing lamps of the dome.
And James sees his bride in the white raiment of the elect,
so bright that the air darkens like thunder about her
and almost his spirit quails, for she has the power
with her she-ness to alter the very texture of his body
as death may do with its alchemical magisterium,
its frightful cookery, but in the other direction.
And she sees him in his black and grey like Death
Himself, the meaning of life, the dignity none
may avoid, the fate that threads all our stories like a spine
of steel; her eyes burn in her pale face
like brandy in cream. But this banquet may not
be tasted, and years must pass before the gate
back into the garden is opened, the princess
awoken, the snow melt away from the frozen paradise.
For after the wedding feast, after the rout of guests
and musicians departed, the white lace laid
in its chest by the fire, the coverlet turned over,
the white dove in the eave having ceased her cooing
and asleep in her nest, the grief is revealed: for Ruth
for all her womanly bosom, her thighs and belly
of silk, her strawberry loveliness set in a cloud
of sugar, her hair ablaze like the sun's gardens,

her sport with her lover Antony, is numb as a scar.
And suddenly James' body seems to her
to be Simon's, the bones and muscles exchanged as if
a devil had taken the disused flesh of a damned
soul, and grafted it onto a hero. And what,
indeed, can this husband do for a helpmeet, who has
no political power, no wealth, from a disgraced family?
And what of her genius, bound to the chariot wheels
of this sombre young emperor, marshal of his own realm of death?
What has she got in this exchange, for her father?
Has she not taken the dark path of her mother?
She looks with terror into the face of the boy
beside her, and strangest of all, he smiles, so kind
that her heart opens; she weeps, having found a friend.
And James, troubled, tender, begins to chuckle,
not as in bitterness, nor lightly, but finding
the world so large, and strange, these two young folk
so at large in the midst of it, carried along for the most part
by quite inappropriate tempests out of the past:
she, shocked by his laughter, looks twice, and sees
the whole point; a great heave passes over her
and she breaks out laughing as well, and falls back, and they both
abandon themselves to the gale of it; anyone there
would think they were mad, and would not see how the grief
was managed and treasured up, set aside for great need
by this shared madness. Do not mistake them,
you who have learned only the notes and the stops of the music,
the common or garden parterres of paradise, coarse
wine and solid nourishment: the tune, the tune,
the evening magic of elms and roses, the bouquet!

◆

But the burned place in her does not recover its feeling:
as if her tongue were cut out, hand's tendons
severed, or as when in certain sicknesses of the brain
the mind cannot feel the words with its fingertips
when it gropes for them, nor lift them to the voice, they are so heavy.
And they go to live at Wolverton Hill Farm,
but Mary Quincy remains at her own insistence
in the rooms above Maple Street in Old Mount Verdant.

At first Shaker McCloud will scarcely speak
with the young man his son-in-law; but James asks
him one day if he would instruct him in certain arts
of battle and management of weapons, for Shaker is famous
for ancient skill in the halberd, longbow, and sword
and possesses a store of arms with microprocessors.
To his own surprise Shaker finds himself saying
"yes" to the young man's request, and next day
they are out in the courtyard, their swords bound
to their waists, exchanging traditional bows. They instruct
their weapons not to bite on the flesh, and fall
to the Samurai stance, each humming a melody
tuned to the minds of their swords. The human ear
can distinguish tones whose vibrations differ only
by microns: a duel between masters of the sword is a duel
of musics, each seeking the pace and the vector
that overreaches his enemy and leaves him naked
to the blade. After a moment or two James
raises the pitch and moves to the left. There's a flash
and the two swords meet and fly apart.
James has expected this, and uses the shock
to power a stroke at the knee. In a moment his sword
is flying over the barn and Shaker's point
hovers an inch from his throat. "Then I do have something
to learn," says James with a smile. Shaker, annoyed,
finds that he likes this boy. The lessons proceed,
and James takes over part of the farm management,
sharing, as is traditional, much of the labor,
coming to know the hands of a hundredth share.

♦

And every night James must swallow the gift
he was to give to his wife, as if it were worthless:
and though he knows he did not create the demons
he has awakened, he also knows he's encountered
a power that throttles and saps his own. That great
spirit in him, that strikes up in his limbs and heart,
the hero-light, naked erect magnanimity,
able to suffer and do, of the man alive
in the world that may kill him—that joy of knowing whatever

answer the world makes to his actions, whether
good or ill, knowing his eight pints of blood,
his strength which in its full is indomitable but which
when its source is smothered, may vanish as happiness does
in the sick; that spirit, the fork of the divine in him,
he feels to droop and draggle and cast itself into
the slough of sloth. And she, seeing how she has wounded
unwilling this grand angel who took her, grieves:
there is no worse grief than to know oneself
to be the agent of death to the thing that one loves,
to lessen to commonplace what one admires. And so,
stealing the keys of her father's armory, she opens
its doors one night and passes within; and she takes
the finest suit of resinite armor and carries it
off to the workshop where she, having suborned
the great goldsmith Matthew Revere to her will,
has him fasten upon the helm, the breastplate, and shield
the golden device she designed for him and commanded
the craftsman to fashion: a ginkgo leaf, as a sign
to him of her love despite the fate of their natures.
And the next day at dinner she stands up before
the polished board and the assembled company, and lays
a bundle wrapped in old silk on the table, and speaks.
"This gift I give to my husband: I stole it away
from my father that I might give it; it is a token
in return for what we have taken from him. Behold!"
And she opens the bundle and holds up the glittering proof.
But Shaker McCloud rises in wrath, and speaks:
"That gift is our honor, and honor cannot be taken
back, lest it break. I concur with the gift, but daughter,
you do not know whence it came. It was made a hundred
years ago in the caves of Hattan by the smith
that some call Kingfish; it is his finest work.
Mohican County in gratitude gave it to Charles
Jefferson, Praetor, for his deeds in the Erie War
when Kelan Riot sought to conquer Sandusky.
But Charles Jefferson was killed by Black County Raiders
and the armor was carried as spoil to Shamokin County.
When Simon Jefferson, the father of Emily Long-Legs
my wife, dwelt in Shamokin County he heard

96

of the armor, saw it, and knew it as that of his grandfather
Charles; and before he returned from Shamokin County
he stole the armor and carried it back. Emily
gave it to me when he died, and I have worn it
in honor to war. That is a great gift:
but I say now that never, whether I be alive
or dead, will the land of George Quincy return
to the Quincys: I had thought to give it when I died, but he
who takes without asking shall not be given that
which is not asked. And since by this act, daughter,
you have declared yourself more a wife than a daughter,
if I cannot punish you for this deed I shall punish
the man that I love whose wife, daughter, you are."

◆

But Ruth herself attires her man in his armor:
the fit is good, but pinches a little at shoulder
and armpit: James takes the cuirass to the workshop
and slowly lasers the white crystalline stuff
to his proper proportion. At last, greaves, cuisses,
gauntlet, visor, and helm, he stands before
his beloved like a man from a myth, anonymous, glittering,
with the dolorous unchanging expression of the war mask's effigy:
but on his breast and his helm the fan-leaves burn.

◆

Very nearly Antony Manse has died,
meanwhile, of the shame and the grief of his loss. But Mungo
his brother-in-law is a friend to him, taking him out
to the fine restaurant on Vine Street and making him
sample the delicate crayfish, the peppered asparagus,
the hearty wild turkey soup, and plying him tactfully
with the fine dry aperitif of the region; Mungo's
a Tory, and they're joined for dinner (a noble rosemaried
shellacked and crumbed rack of lamb) by the poet Elvira,
her brother Christopher, "Galloping Jack" Sherman,
and two or three others, all of them party veterans.
The subject turns to the threat of the Mad Counties:
the new Messiah has stirred up the Fundamentalists
from V'mont to Giniah, bringing together a dozen

different sects and healing their schisms. News
of burnings and mass self-mutilation, massacres,
even the total obliteration of Delphia Riot—
and then the bad tidings from the West—have set
the party the problem of whether to sink their differences,
joining the Whigs, as they have requested, in forming
a coalition; or to fight with vigor the upcoming election;
or to settle into the role of loyal opposition.
The upshot is that they'll fight the election, but need
the strongest and likeliest candidate: in a word, Antony.
A war hero, scion of the Manse family,
army major, and popular figure in sport,
they want him to run for elector and then for the Senate.
The Whigs believe in a strong militia, distrust
the army professionals, stand for defense and non-
provocation; the Tories want an aggressive diplomacy
backed up by crack regular army forces
prepared to act preemptively outside their borders.
The Whigs represent the Brahmin ideology;
the Tories are led by Kshatriyas. But many warriors
go with the Whigs, and most of the Vaisyas: the farmers
usually vote for the Tories, though there's a strong
Whig minority among the devout farmers
of the North. Now there's a chance for the Tories to win
the election and send an expeditionary force—
spiked with Tuscarawans smarting for revenge
and eager to get back their land—to deal a blow
to the hosts of the new Messiah, giving us time
to deal with the menace of the West. Antony Manse,
an old campaigner, is caught, and in these intrigues
forgets for a while the pain of defeat. But soon
he must find himself working side by side with a colleague
running for office as he is, and on the same ticket:
Ruth Jefferson Quincy, the bride that he lost.

◆

The agony of suffering's much like the anguish of joy:
James George Quincy has never known pain
so terrible, though everything outward goes on as usual:
a pain that's so huge it's taken on the proportions

98

of apocalypse, of a rolling back of the clouds to reveal
a brightness that penetrates every commonplace object
with brilliant life; when he wakes in the morning, for a moment
it's almost as if he'd forgotten some secure delight
like a Christmas present, and must search back to discover
again what it is that has changed everything utterly.
And then he recalls, and the gift is a grief so perfect
nothing can ever distract him; yet he lives his life,
is an excellent farmer and manager, practices weapons
with Shaker, finds in his wife a deeper and deeper
beauty and power of sensibility, a freedom
of laughter and friendship that carries the high halcyon
light of noble disinterest, cut off entirely
as it is from the mutilate stump of love and the corpse
of physical tenderness. What is worst of all is that James
knows that it's he in particular, the very force
of his love and desire, that freezes the gates shut
of her sweetness and walls up alive in numb flesh
the infant of happiness. His soul twists like a snake
that has bitten itself and now has spasmed itself
out of its skin with the impossible ache of the venom.
And in public they are so happily married; indeed
not a word passes between them of complaint or reproach:
Ruth refuses to consult a doctor or priest,
knowing her fate come upon her and having no wish
to shirk it or fall into debt to another, especially
one whom she feels to be her inferior: the armor
she gives to her husband is a dearer gift than her flesh.
But such greatness of pain and will and clarity
of spirit burns up the powers of endurance we need
to resist the wearing of time: however perfect,
a human act prolonged at such cost cramps
and enfeebles the muscles of motive and self-reward.
You who listen to this my poem, reflect:
it is easy to suffer in splendor the light of tragedy—
all that it takes is the hero's art of abandon—
and any philosophy teaching the knack of detachment
is trivial, the bien-pensant boast of a boy,
when set against that pain incurred by attachment
to what we ought indeed to be attached to,

99

when that which we love is slowly destroyed by our love.
I sing in this poem what recourse offers itself
in this case, what is the uttermost gift we can offer.

2. The Death of the Father

Ruth's gift to James of the armor, she knows,
is the wrong gift: he wanted only herself;
and in sign of its error, James has thereby lost
the last chance to get back the lands of his father.
And every day she is down at the party headquarters
or speaking in public, fighting the Whig candidate,
a sanctimonious fellow who trusts the good faith
of the Mad Counties, "if we sit down and reason together."
And she fears he will win, for the amateur soldiers who fill
the militia are thirsty for Kshatriya glory, and the farmers
and Vaisyas are afraid that war will disrupt the market.
But in due course she encounters Antony Manse
at a policy meeting, and such are the needs of the moment
that he and she are thrown together to work
on the same policy task force. The old friendship
revives, and with it the easy, natural desire.
One day they are sent to Mansfield and stay
in the same pretty hotel where once they were lovers.
That night each lies alone,
listening to blues from the bar over the street;
in the morning they both know the thoughts of the other,
and Antony's face is so sad she grieves for him; hers
is to him, in its yearning, its flush and its glances flashing
away, the sleepwarmth still in her limbs, a flown
flag of desire. But now a high cold
spirit blows in her; the breath of an act of generosity
splendid and terrible, to last for a thousand years.
And she quits the campaign that moment, and cares not
that her name cannot now be removed from the ballot, and rides
to Wolverton Hill, and (all the actress of the neglected
child coming out in her) feigns a sudden warmth,

a change of heart that she does not feel; James
is suspicious, knowing the greatness and subtlety of her nature,
but after two weeks he is sure that mysteriously
the clogged ice has melted, and that it was time
only that Ruth had needed, to forget the act
of Simon Raven McCloud and grow into marriage.
And in three nights of consummate art she makes
him believe he is loved and desired to the point of tears;
and in his life of endurance and hope denied
he has never known such happiness, lightness of heart,
sweetness each day coming like the smell of dawn
and the scent of roses in through the window, the trellised
convolvulus, long grass by the river, apples
and honey and the sun on the hot straw, blue
hilltops blazing against the horizon, the honey,
the honey. He has been given a living heart,
he has been given a person's own self. What
does he have to give in return, to his lovely long person,
his old Penelope? With what may he ward off
the ill-luck of his happy stars? What juice,
what inwardness, beyond the tender, body's
gasp of inner butter? What mead of the soul?
He has given to her, though she does not know it, a son;
and it's all a noble pretense, a sacrifice, an act
of supreme generosity. What is the truth in this world?
Should we wish to know what is behind
the appearances of things? Indeed, is there anything behind them?

◆

On the third day the elections are held. The County
has its strange gala revolution, as democracies do,
where leaders and governments are overthrown without bloodshed,
then settles down for a night of fireworks and parties,
as losers and winners weep and join in celebration.
Ruth has scarcely followed the results and remains
at home; the retainers go in to Mount Verdant to drink:
but her mother's nurse, Barbara, stays behind,
and when the results are announced she hurries to Ruth
who is sitting before the fire with James, silent.
By a small margin Ruth has won, and is an elector.

101

Shaker has kept his seat and will likely be senator;
Antony, too, has the victory: the Tories have swept
the county, a new age is beginning. Ruth,
to her own surprise, bursts into tears: to be so
trusted, and held by the people as worthy to serve them
brings back the whole pride of her kin and nurture.
That same day Shaker, for the first
time, has met his match by the sword, for in practice
with James he had found at last no flaw in his defense,
and so swift and subtle had James' attack proved to be,
that Adamant had not been able to stay his stroke
but had cut a light flesh wound in Shaker's right arm.
Nevertheless Shaker, delighted, had seized
the young man in a mighty hug, and called him his son:
the old man rests upstairs in his library
with a brandy, a video, a sheaf of congressional reports.

◆

But now, to the southwest, a redness grows
in the sky. Ruth and James see it from the window;
and a few minutes later Billy Blubaugh,
the bailiff of Lithend Farm, rides up at a gallop.
"The barn is on fire! Come quick! It'll spread to the house!"
It is the old wooden barn from the twentieth century
restored by George Quincy thirty years earlier.
Had the elections not carried away the retainers
Shaker would send every man and woman, but stay
at Wolverton Hill himself to look after his own;
now, he is eager to go himself, but James
advises him gently to stay because of his wound,
and he and Ruth ride off to help at the fire.
Other neighbors have come, and it's almost a bonfire,
though people are pouring water, not fuel, on the flames:
the blaze is controlled, but the barn is apparently lost
by the time morning begins its own irresistible
fire in the eastern sky. The Quincys return
in a mood of gaiety undergirded with grief:
James for what he has lost, and Ruth for her part in it.

◆

But when they come back to the house there is no welcome:
the place is silent and dark, and they burst inside
to discover the hall floor wet with slippery
liquid, a metallic smell in the air, and death
in the house. The old nurse lies in the doorway,
her throat cut from ear to ear; beyond
are the corpses of four or five men, dressed in black
and bearing insignias showing the fiery cross
of the Mad Counties, and a new sign, a black
bird edged in crimson, a raven flying.
Beyond them lies Shaker, his sword in his hand, his chest
battered through with a laser bolt; he has bled all over the room.
"They set the fire in the barn to draw off our people,"
says James quietly, "but did not know they were gone
for the night. If I had not wounded him, Shaker your father
would have escaped. Ruth, my love, my queen,
this is my fault and I must avenge it." And Ruth,
ignoring the gouts of blood that are soaking her clothes,
embraces her father's head, and coughs and moans.
James kneels down by her, holds her tightly,
while with the other hand he closes the eyes
of the old man; he bends and kisses his forehead
and smooths the shock of white hair. "And now I must leave,"
says James: "Give me my armor." She stands at last,
and together they fetch the armor and buckle it on.
James takes up his own father's sword, kisses it,
binds it about his waist. By now it is day
and the first stragglers from dance or carouse are beginning
to wind up the path. He saddles Shaker's horse,
a grey named Gringolet after the mount of the hero,
tells Ruth to send any men she finds to follow,
and rides away east like a storm. By noon he knows
his guess was correct, for at Coshocton he hears
from the local police that ten mounted men passed through
in white cloaks, claiming that they were the bearers
of battle plans for a new attack in the east.
James knows that under the cloaks is black
armor, and he rides on into Tuscarawas
by the same route that the hunters took when they sought
the outlaw Simon McCloud four years ago.

103

♦

He catches them early that evening, camped by the shores
of Tappan Lake, and awaiting a flatboat to ferry
them over when night will conceal them from Free
County patrols. All day his fury
has simmered within him and now it bursts forth like lava
or hot acid burning his heart and his bowels:
in the last months he's come to love Shaker as a father
and something inside him refuses to believe in the change
that's come over his wife; it is as if the enemy
stood for the thing in her that withered at his approach.
He is dry from long riding, and his voice, when he calls, is a scream
scarcely the sound of a man, commanding his enemy
to turn and defend themselves. They, seeing a single
horseman, are puzzled, and then break out into laughter:
the tallest one mounts, and charges up the slope,
a black pennon bearing the sign of the raven
blurred by the speed at his lance point; James, armed
only with sword and shield, deflects the lance
and smashes his enemy's horse with the flat of the blade
so that the beast is stunned, and falls, and its rider
sprawls in the grass. Below, James can see
the long lake lit with the lime and ochre
and sallow crimson of evening, calm as a millpond:
a point of hard sand going out in a cusp, and on it,
nine men struggling to arm and to mount.
He screams again "Aoi!" and charges at once:
The onset is fierce, and one rider is split
from the crown of his head to his breastbone; he'd forgotten his helmet:
another is struck from his horse, and stunned: the rest
are on foot, but ready now for a battle. James
dismounts, and again without pausing, his rage seeming
to lighten his steps but turning his arms and his breast
into giants' members, his breath to the pant of a furnace,
he rushes the enemy. Two more, the joints
in their armor pierced by the cunning of Adamant, fall:
the marvelous armor of Ruth, fluted and shining,
spins off one blade and stops another one dead.
Now they close in about him; he is suddenly cool,

and seeing their caution, is moved to laugh in his turn;
and he feels so young, and immortal, and lost, here
under the sky of Ahiah, where waterbirds dip
and the fine sand crunches under his step.
At his laugh they hesitate, wondering; in that moment
he strikes, the croon of his song to the sword matched
to the swooping whine of the blade. A man falls,
and with his shield James bullies another
till he stumbles into the lake. Now his enemies,
terrified, wish to escape; but he has them before him
with their backs to the water, and slowly advances, the ginkgo
leaves on his armor and helmet burning like torches.
One of them tries to get past; with a blow James
decapitates him, and, spinning, meets the charge of the others.
The sword, at point, pierces the armor of one
and transfixes him; but the weapon is torn from the hands of the hero
and now, with a roar, James throws himself bodily
upon the survivors. One of them, though he is armed,
cannot control his sphincters, and fouls himself, runs
away in his madness, trips on a stone, and smashes
an ankle; the other is able to find the chink
in the cuirass and sink his blade home. James, with his last
strength, seizes the man by the middle, and breaking
the straps, rips off his helmet and throttles him. Horror
suddenly falls on the hero: he sits on the sand
and doffs his own helmet. But the first rider, remounted,
charges him now; he rolls from the hooves, recovers
his sword, and turns to meet his assailant; who,
looming like fate, with a gesture raises his visor.
In the last light James can see it is Simon
himself. "Brother, you dare to lift your hand
to the Messiah: for this blasphemy you are sentenced to die."
But James, fainting with weariness, loss of blood,
growls in his throat and charges. His thrust pierces
the groin of his enemy, but Simon's stroke has fallen
sidelong across his face and James, stunned
by the blow, cannot see. There's shouting above:
the other pursuers have come. Simon curses,
reins in his horse. Blinded, James flails
with his sword. "Why do you call me brother?" he cries.

105

Simon does not reply, but spurs his horse,
and gallops away along the edge of the sand;
night conceals him, and soon his pursuit is despaired of.
Old Billy Blubaugh orders a fire to be built
and sends for a doctor; gently he tends his young master.

3. A Funeral and a Council

James is carried back raving, blind, in a fever;
will not allow Ruth to come near him, but struggles
whenever he hears the sound of her voice: nor endure
the presence of even his mother; so Catherine McCloud,
Ruth's sister, is called from her house in the city
where in a pretty room she divines the afflictions
of desperate folk; she is asked to nurse the fallen
hero, and assist the doctors to bring back the light
to his eyes. Doctor Mercurius, of the same Brahmin
family as the man Ruth defeated for office
but who, like many doctors who accept the currency
of obligation to perform their services, has taken
the caste of Vaisya, attends at James' bedside:
but nothing can be done, he says, till the fever abates
and that shall not be till the troubled mind is calm
and the spirit at peace with itself. Again and again
James cries out, "Who is my brother? Who
is my mother? Who is my father? Who is my sister?"
—but no one may reason with him, and nobody answers
the riddle he asks, and his face, though healed of its wound,
leaving only a scar on the cheek and the brow, stares
sightless forever. Catherine divines and divines,
but there is a shadow over the past, and a great brightness
over the future, that turns to shadow again without losing
its brightness. At last, on Catherine's advice, the monk
her brother, Robert McCloud, who is now named
Brother Siddhartha, is called in to help. Meanwhile
the funeral of Shaker McCloud is solemnly celebrated:
all the great folk of the county are there, but five

who were murdered like Shaker in this last raid; and many
of the little who loved Shaker McCloud for his gifts
and his power and wise advice, and his generalship
in battles long ago. A dais of stone
is set up in the midst of the wide west field
of Wolverton Hill Farm, and on it a pyre
of sweet-smelling timber—rare cedar, oak,
well-seasoned pine with the sap standing like jewels
at crotch and at cut; beautiful silvery billets
of beech and of maple, and boughs of memorial yew;
around are the cairns—also of finely dressed sandstone
so fitted that mortar is needless and a knife may not enter
the cracks—of two centuries of McCloud dead.
On the new cairn the casket is laid, a bier
of simple white oak, unvarnished, and over it thrown
the great beautiful quilt that Emily McCloud
slew herself on, and over the quilt in turn
the flag of Mohican County—white, with a tree of gold
bearing both golden flowers and apples of gold.
In the kitchen the cook and the maids and servingmen rush
hither and thither in panic; a barrel of wine
from the valley of Les Tres Riches Heures is broached;
the pyre is lit by Ruth, Mungo, and Catherine,
grieving, while Robert-Siddhartha prays with the priest
from Mount Verdant Cathedral. It is a hot day,
the purple-blue sky of Ahiah smudged with the smoke,
and the flames hot but almost invisible; Mungo
breaks open, as ritual demands, the skull of his father
as the flames die down, and Catherine pours the wine,
honey, and milk on the flames from beautiful vessels,
and Ruth carries the cumbersome sword of Shaker
McCloud to break its temper in the fire, be reforged
for the scabbard of Mungo McCloud. After the pyre,
the ashes and bones will be set in an urn and buried
under the cairn, and an apple tree planted; the mourners
return to the house for the feast. Great swine
and beeves have been slaughtered, and sauces of corn and cream
tempered to nap their brilliant shellacked flanks;
bass and bream are borne in, smoking with butter
and winey steam; salads of endive and radish

and cress, and suave custards and caramels with lemons
and oranges shipped up the river from fantastic Floridy.

♦

But Brother Siddhartha comes to James in the evening
and does not speak, but sits cross-legged on the floor
and meditates an hour. Since his devout boyhood,
his face has changed—not, strangely, to the mask of the ascetic,
but to the jolly bearded visage of a Santa Claus
or a Ganesha or some local Kami of millet
or rice wine. The life of denial sometimes
has this effect: as if renunciation
restored the world to a man from within when it's lost
to the outward person. The monk's soul pursues
and at last yields to the darkness of Yahman; his breath
disappears, and an immense calm grows in the sickroom.
And now James' restless writhing begins
to abate, and after a while both men
are as still, it seems, as the great man recently
laid to rest. Out of the silence comes a voice,
so kind and matter-of-fact that madness would seem
so out of place as not to be applicable. "James.
Simon called you brother, didn't he? Why
not? You're his sister's husband, after all."
James is still; but suddenly gives a long sigh.
"He meant something else, I am sure of it. Something my mother—
if she is my mother—will not tell, whether
mistakenly wishing to spare me, or to protect
the memory of my father—if he is my father—or else
she wishes to have this power of a secret over me. Who is it
can tell me who I am?" Siddhartha stretches, smiles,
comes over and sits on the bed. "Look at it this way,"
he says. "You've just found out the truth about everyone.
Everyone screws himself to get born, everyone's
always his own great-grandpa. And if that isn't enough
we're also our grandmas and mothers and aunts and always
our brother and always a stranger unto ourselves.
Consider a family of sisters and brothers: if the first
had come second, he'd not be the man he became, for the first
would already have taken the role. Or twins—did you know

108

that when they are raised apart they're more, not less
like each other? This is the wisdom of Yahman: our star
is the shit of the stars, our bodies the shit of the world.
And our souls; what may any misfortune do
unto them, being made, as the future is, out of the void
and akin to it, sharing its invulnerability? Be calm."
And as at another time James had likewise
been struck to the soul by the sheer comedy of it all,
so now, he begins to chuckle; in the cool of the breaking
fever, he discovers a tickle of the mind so fierce
that he rocks with laughter, shaking, sitting up in his bed
and slapping the monk on the back, staring at him
with no surprise that he can suddenly see again;
though he finds at once, by the absence of fringes and ghosts
in the field of sight, and also the absence of depth,
with one eye only. And he knows, too,
without grief or commotion, that Ruth has feigned those three
moments of joy, and that nothing needs to have meaning.

◆

There's a meaning in nothing, as James swiftly learns,
in two different senses. A week later,
the will and testament of Shaker McCloud are read
in the great hall to the family and all the retainers.
James is well enough now to sit in a chair
and here in person. The bequests to the hands and servants
are generous; as they expect, Mungo and Catherine
get most of the goods and the valuables; Ruth has been left
the bulk of the land, but Shaker, not wishing to burden
his daughter with his own dead identity, allows
the County to take back the currency he has amassed
through his deeds of assistance and mighty works for his neighbors.
The meaning of nothing now becomes plain: "To James
my son-in-law, whom I love beyond all other men,
though I found him late and unwillingly, my honor and his
require that I leave him nothing: that was our compact.
But nevertheless I bequeath him my blessing and prophecy:
he shall attain in the end to his heart's desire."
Lithend Farm he disposes of thus: "To the man
whom I sought for my son, Antony Manse, I give

the farm at Lithend that belonged once to George
Quincy the father of James; let him not give it
nor yield it away except to one that he loves
more than himself. —Being of sound mind
and body this Election Day twenty-three hundred
and eighty, I set my hand and seal to this testament;
Shaker McCloud, Senator, Praetor once
to the Sovereign County Mohican, marshal and general
serving the people of the County, Judge, Master
of Wolverton Hill Farm." So the ink was scarcely
dry on the paper the night that Shaker had died.

♦

The other meaning of nothing he learns a month later.
Friendship, respect only have passed between Ruth
and James in the last weeks. For certain signs
Ruth consults a doctor; the marvelous medicine
of the twenty-fourth century finds she is bearing a boy,
healthy, perfect, and normal, though hardly yet
to be seen by the eye. This news Ruth
tells to her husband. And just as the legacy left him
by Shaker McCloud had carried a double load,
so these tidings are twisted within themselves, shaped
by interpretation to lead what life in public
they may. As Jesus said, the tares are sowed
with the corn: every particle that springs into life
is twinned with its negative: each is the same light
flashing reflected from opposite sides of the wave
of the present, and were they to meet, they should instantly vanish
to zero, whence, because nothing has meaning, they came.
The universe takes its beginning in incest: to know
is carnal knowledge, to be is to be known.
But James finds in despair a kind of happiness
and heals grimly, the right eye full of light
but the left dark as if it had never seen.

♦

In pain with his wound, but driven not by the flesh,
Simon rides back alone into Allegany:
the twelve peers he appointed, slain or captured

behind him, and their squires also, all as he
had intended. For four of the peers were sons of the Elders
of Allegany, Shamokin, Susquehanna, and Monongahela:
the others, holy princes themselves, the flower
of Black County leadership. The goal of their raid—
the death of the warlords of the Free Counties—was merely
part of Simon's intention: for the death of his followers
serves the cause of his power as much as the death
of his enemies. Only Shaker McCloud was essential
for revenge and his own satisfaction. For now, after years
of talk, of the display of charisma, the hellish or heavenly
confidence that wins questioning folk to your love;
of wandering village fairs, and preaching to multitudes;
getting the ear of the Elders, fashioning legends
that mark the mystical crown of the true Messiah;
of words that turn pity and love of the poor into knives,
that take the milky sweetness of motherhood, softness
of babies, and wifely and husbandly tenderness, turn them
to acid rage against those you conceive their enemies;
of building a war machine, an alliance stretching
across the mountains and plains; the attempt to convert
the Delphia Riot that failed, but cemented the Counties
Crusading, by making them share in the holocaust, the city
sacked, babies in rubbery heaps in the streets,
mothers ripped from the nether lips to the plexus,
boys and men made to eat their own genitals,
the scream that crowned over the city like fire—
that act could not be turned back: if religion
failed to justify that, then nothing could wipe off
the guilt, and failure to continue that course would imply
that something perhaps was amiss—after all this,
after the hard political work, Simon
is ready to reap the fruit of his rage and patience,
and ride back alone, without rivals, to take up his Godhead.

◆

As soon as the new government of Mohican County
has come into power, it calls a council, bringing
the wisest of both the parties, and the County's leaders
in every caste and all the arts and sciences

111

together to moot the matter of war. Ruth,
in the press of time, is called to stand for her father;
Antony Manse and James George Quincy
(who wears a black patch over his eye)
are there as aides to General Moira Gioia,
and Claudius Manse, and General Jack Sherman,
and the abbot Padmasambhava, and Professor Basileus,
and Maury "Skip" Edsel, who's settled in Mohican
and now runs a shipping empire throughout
the Great Lakes, and his friend Douglas McCloud
the airship wizard, and Camilla McCloud, and Catherine
the diviner, and many others. Elizabeth Madison,
Praetor, formally opens the meeting with news
from the Free Counties throughout the East and Central
Uess: the future has not looked darker since the days
of the Great Pogrom against the middle class,
when Elizabeth, the present Praetor's namesake, broke
with the Cumbus Riot and led her people to freedom.
Several senators speak; technical testimony
is invited from the Chiefs of Staff. Mohican's forces
are small but finely equipped, and their quality, fire,
and morale are unequaled anywhere. But against such numbers
the best hope of defense is to delay the collapse
for a couple of years, and to make the enemy pay
by a last stand that will perhaps be recorded
in song, if there are any left to sing it.
"Then," says Jack Sherman, "Let us give up hope:
And let these three centuries of light speak
for themselves; we show our fidelity by selling our lives
at the rate they deserve. Perhaps it's time to draw
down the curtain: no civilization endures forever.
Let us make of ourselves a fortress and let us live finest
of all, our hearts higher, our mood the more,
as our might lessens. What though the light be spent?
It burned highest, let them say, at its quenching;
Let us overmatch their hatred with our despair."
"The words of a soldier," says Septimus Adams, the leader
of the Whig opposition, a Brahmin and scholar; "and I warrant
a good soldier indeed, who must cast himself into
a kind of despair when he charges the enemy. But we

must work with a world that continues, and find our way,
however demeaning, among the mazes of political
fact and reality. Let us negotiate carefully,
waiting for help, conserving the lives of those
that we love and not enraging the enemy by spilling
his blood and whetting his thirst for revenge." "I agree,"
says Charlie Layman the farmer, "if you're willing to bow
to their priests and elders and give up our art of faith
for a black coat and a book of hellfire and brimstone.
For me, it don't make much difference; I'll plow my east field
in spring come what may, and think my own thoughts: but my boys
will learn to think like a slave, and I'd see them die
first, rather than lose the devil in their eyes,
the rooster and mustard and sass that the profs call freedom."
"Perhaps we can buy them," says Skip. "Give them some ships
and some money, and bribe the officials, and show them some life
high on the hog, and get the women wearing
the fashions, and rouse up the ones on the bottom with stories
hyping the high life of the bosses, and slip 'em
a bit of civilized sex, and work 'em around
with wine, and get their youngsters on joyjuice
and wait for the whole crazy thing to collapse."
"That would work, I think," says Professor Basileus,
"If things were as they once were. But now their Messiah
is better to them than sighs of passion, wine,
envy, fashion, and sweets. And what should we do
to ourselves if we took such a course? Better, I think,
to be a Mad Countian, which is at least
to be human, than a Rioter, and even *their* lives
we respect; worst of all to become a Burbian,
cowardice pander to violence and lust. But I thank
the merchant, whose grasp of history betters that
of most of the rest of us. Let me call my student Ruth
to speak for her father: what would Shaker advise?"
"He would, I think," she says, "give us a choice.
First, we could simply pull up and leave. The County
is rich; even now we could sell our land to the Mad
Countian farmers; cash in our offworld currencies;
buy ourselves five interstellar shells, and go.
It might be a worthy thing for our folk to do:

113

to build a new world somewhere in the stars."
"How can you say such a thing?" asks Antony Manse,
impassioned: "Let their Messiah take all? Vile,
dishonorable submission! And leave our friends and allies?
Let the planet, where the race of Humankind learned
its divine power of speech, pass into darkness?
Consider, friends—and forgive me, a soldier, blunt
in the ways of councils—consider the cornfields by Bellville,
shining in the sun. Consider the valley of Les Tres
Riches Heures. Consider our capital, old
Mount Verdant, under the snow; the Cathedral,
peach blossoms in spring, the barley mow,
the apples of Mohican County in all the Septembers,
and all the Ahian summers of long ago."
"The question, splendid young man," says Professor Basileus,
"is what, when evil exists, we should do with it.
Many would say, leave it to itself, and let it
afflict itself, and let us not be touched by it.
But speak, Ruth McCloud Quincy, what
is the last choice that Shaker McCloud would offer?"
"Defense," says Ruth slowly, "is, if our warriors
speak wisely, only a means of delaying the end.
And now my father, I think, is speaking within me.
If we cannot defend ourselves, let us attack. The Jihad
feeds on its own seizing of fate to itself:
it thinks itself the force that determines the world,
and deals only with itself, burning like fire
in the forest, blown by its own momentum. Let us fight
fire with fire; let us seize the quick of the moment
before they have time to breathe, and smite them maliciously;
when they see that events do not fall as they prophesy, when instead
of a fierce defense, which is what they expect, they see us
carelessly fly against them as if it were we
that held the advantage, when they know our courage and anger
hotter and quicker than theirs, they will be cowed
and fall into confusion; perhaps even
they will slay their Messiah. Such has happened before.
And now I see I have two weapons (so Shaker
would word it) that I can throw against the Jihad:
two terrible weapons, though it would cost me dear

114

if they should be broken; and to the east a great mine
which if it should burst, might fearfully wound the Jihad."
"You speak wisely but darkly, young woman," says the Praetor
Elizabeth; "What is your mine and what are these weapons?"
"The mine, my lady, is the County of Tuscarawas:
they of the green armor are a proud folk
of a line as ancient as we. And their lands,
as we know, have been held for years by the men of the black.
If they should be roused, and armed with our help, they'd burst
on the Black Counties like a storm." "And the two weapons?"
"You have heard from one of them only a moment ago:
Antony Manse, who has his own reasons for hating
the man who now bears the name of Messiah; Antony
proved his wrath in the battle of St. Clair. Of that battle
another man lived to speak: my husband, James,
whom I give to the County as my greatest and most precious
possession: he it was that defeated ten men
in the late raid, and his sword has tasted the blood
of Simon Raven, and he hates him for reasons secret
and terrible. These two weapons we have,
and they will vie each with the other which
will prove the most bloody and cunning against the enemy.
They are polished and heavy, my lords, ladies and citizens:
be glad their edges are aimed in another direction."
The Council, almost persuaded by this, is inclined
to take the desperate course that Ruth recommends;
but much debate follows. At length they agree, and turn
to James and Antony, "Are you as resolute, bloody,
and full of despair as your spokeswoman says?" Antony
merely inclines his head; but James will speak.
"Indeed, I care not a pin for my life; but I pity
the soldiers I lead and the folk I shall slay. If
it be possible, let this cup pass away from me; yet not
my will, but yours be done." The Council
votes to call up all the reserves, to create
two swift mounted forces, supplied
by the sunplane squadrons, manned by elite volunteers,
and placed in contact with all the Mohican spies;
each shall contain two thousand men, and be sent
into Vaniah at once on a mission of ravage and terror.

One shall be led by Antony, the other by James.
Meanwhile the allies will meet in a week: Tuscarawas
has asked for a promise to get back the land that it lost,
and the promise now will be given, together with arms
and an army: Sandusky and Wyandot asked to hold on
till the war in the east is won, and the Free Counties
can turn their strength to the west. The whole county
falls to work at the preparations of war;
for ten days scarcely anyone sleeps;
dirigibles stuffed with weapons bought with the good
credit of the County from Rockwell and General Electric
drone in along the traditional routes;
all personal obligations are canceled,
the money so raised to be used for the cost of the war.
Antony's force will be named the Spear, for the spear
wherewith he slew the great Boar; but Ruth embroiders
into the banner of James the sign of the Bee
to stand for the trial of patience by which he won her.
His soldiers call him One-Eyed Jago; so James,
George, Rollo, has got himself a new name.

4. The Battle of Harrisburg

Like hawks that are flung at a great crane or heron,
the two Mohican battalions are flung at the East.
It has been put about that the busy preparations
are all for a last-stand defense, that a detachment of troops
will be sent to Tuscarawas to strengthen its lines.
Some of the attack forces go openly by road;
the rest, with James, travel at night in the woods
and farmlands, a hundred or so at a time. It's summer;
the day lilies riot in hedgerow and wayside,
in the forest dells there's the faint fragrance of sweet
rocket, and lemon balm crushed, and wild mint
in the eaves of the woods where a fence keeps off the sheep.
Careful plans have been laid; in Tuscarawas
they're joined by a couple of thousand irregulars who know

116

the country well, having been ousted after
the truce from their lands. They slip over the border
into Monongahela and Allegany, in groups;
their strategy always the sudden attack, choosing
especially training camps, centers of supply and communication,
officers' quarters, everything thought most secure;
then retreat when the enemy gathers his force to retaliate,
striking at columns of reinforcements, sometimes
grouping several companies in battalion strength
for a pitched battle when all the conditions are favorable
and the enemy's fully outnumbered; always they act
as if their numbers were greater; attack from the east
and retreat in the same direction; live off the land
and resupply from whispering sunplanes evading
the enemy radars; join up with partisans
from the enslaved Free Counties of Vaniah. There are failures
of course; whole platoons trapped and slain
to the last soldier; a few men and women
captured and crucified; but the plan begins to succeed.
James and Antony meet in a cave on the slopes
of Mahantango Mountain in the heart of Shamokin County
and decide the time is ripe for the next phase
of the war. Tuscarawas must strike now
to recover its lands; a day or so later Antony's
force of the Spear must attack the seat of the Messiah
himself in Harrisburg, where the main force of the Jihad
is preparing under the eye of their master. If all
goes well, that force will be weakened by loss of a division
sent to the west to cope with the Tuscarawans,
and depleted further by various regiments sent
to hold vital centers against the Mohican raiders.
A large part of the troops remaining should follow
the force of the Spear when it flees, and fall into ambush
set by the force of the Bee. Perhaps the Messiah
himself will be there, and with luck will be caught by a bolt
from a Free Countian sharpshooter. James and Antony,
rivals and enemies home in their native land,
are brothers now in the cave; they roll up the maps
and their aides bring them flagons of wine; they toast
each other and drink, old campaigners muddy

and ragged, rain pouring outside the mouth
of the cave, and dripping from ferns. "To Ruth Quincy,"
says Antony, raising his glass. "To Ruth Quincy."

♦

But no mere Black County preacher
nor petty paladin, whipped up with hellfire and positive
thinking, nor snake handler, nor layer-on of hands
to the credulous, nor potentate praising the lord for his thousands,
nor sly politician kissing the parish babies
was he who had forged an empire out of these tribes,
Simon Raven McCloud, the Prophesied, He
who came once in gentleness, dying once on the Cross,
but who came now in wrath, the Reaper of Corn,
the Divine Tornado, the Scourge of Delphia Riot,
King of Kings, Lord of Lords, from Eternity
dwelling in blackness there in the Breast of the Lord,
the Razor of God, the Eclipse, the Black Hole
of salvation, uprooter of the cock of filthiness, gouger
of the cunt of sensuality: He to whom virgins are brought
on the eve of marriage, that never, all of their lives
might they pleasure in flesh nor forget the fire of the Lord;
He to whom it is given to grant rest
to men, and release them from the burden of their lives. No
mere measures of men might disturb his serenity,
for now he has come alive from the land of the infidel
when all about him were slain, his people have greeted him
city by city, confraternities vying
which should give him the greatest honor, with girls
in white dresses, green ribbons, boys
carrying green pine branches, babies
held out by the Mothers of the Moral Majority for blessing;
now in his triumph the Lord had almost forgotten
that other life he led before the moment
when unto him was revealed his mission and godhood,
the dark dream out of which he came: the death
of the woman that bore him; banishment at the hands of him
he had thought his father; his training in spells by Faith
his grandmother; the woman he loved who denied him and must,
in the day of his victory, be torn before him by dogs.

118

He sees the plans of his enemies; the blind hosts
that toil under his command are nothing to him, instruments
of his revenge; let his old friends James and Antony
slaughter a few thousand of his men, if they can;
if not, his orders are capture, not death; the mind
of his foes he would break, not their bodies. A prize
greater than any before awaits the Messiah
if his enemies gain the victory in coming battle:
that victory he will turn to the scourge and terror
of the Lord, as pay and punishment for their failure in Delphia:
he will convert the Riots by the fire of his followers,
and turn them into a weapon to rule the world.
Faith is a drug sweeter than honey, sweeter
even than tenderness, sweeter than joyjuice, sweeter
than life itself. Give faith to the Riots and all
shall be changed, all shall be utterly changed. He smiles,
lying upon the great square bed
of lapis lazuli, silver, and silk in the black
marble presence chamber under a canopy
of stars, where he is wont to receive the ambassadors.

♦

The attack on Harrisburg takes place a week later.
That the assault be convincing, it must be pressed fiercely.
Two companies of volunteers are consecrated, their names
recorded for the monument before Mount Verdant Cathedral;
on the eve of the battle they are feted by their comrades, who bring
them wild flowers and garland them over, and serve them
with wine and the choicest cuts of roasted meat;
now a few of them cannot hold their resolve, but repent:
their comrades treat them with gentle kindness, allow them
to go with honor to their tents. The rest are given
at dusk the choice of which lover they will, man
or woman, from the ranks of their friends. That night
the army of the Spear camps in the pines about Piketown;
the morning is misty, clearing to hot and bright
as they ride for Harrisburg along the Fredericksburg road.
Before noon they have reached the outskirts; the enemy
gives no sign. Antony, fearing a trap,
probes forward and extends his line on the flanks.

Ahead in the distance he sees the square monolith
of the Holy of Holies, the Black Temple, with its golden
cupola, vast as a snow-hill, shining in the sun:
about it, he knows, lies a complex of barracks and armories
fenced by a wall. Twelve thousand men,
he estimates, are left in Harrisburg: his forces are outnumbered
six to one. He chuckles, recalling James'
principle of minority attack: "You cannot lose."
Antony gives orders; rockets are unlimbered, their Mikes
instructed as lovingly as human volunteers:
Antony prepares a great sacrilege. At a word
the rockets spring like athletes from their tubes, and streak
in a weaving line, close over the ground,
vault over buildings and walls, and with ruthless intention
fly for the targets that they see with their silicon eyes
and choose with their fierce suicidal minds as matching
best with the words of their loved masters. In a fountain
of violet smoke the great cupola collapses;
armories sink and rise up again for a brief
recrudescence as the stored explosives ignite into noon.
At the same moment the probe encounters resistance;
lasers flash and there is a mutter of thunder.
They ride back in haste as behind them a host
arises, a dark cloud on the horizon, their pennons
of black like a forest floating above them, their hooves
like the onset of earthquake, the roar of the holy tornado.
But the two companies, named Lily and Rose
for the wild flowers that trail from their helms, burst
at this, into song, and form a line of white
to counter the black; and Antony weeps, and raises
his sword in salute, and lets them go. As a shard
of phosphorus dropped in a dish of water, the element
that would, if it could, quench, but ignites the metal;
as the blow of a lover that rouses the ardor still higher;
as the lightning that burns a track in the darkest cloud,
so the white line of the Lily and Rose, led
by a brother and sister, Gareth and Eleanor Madison,
bursts into a flame of swords at the impact
and slips through the ranks of the enemy like a hot wire
through butter. But meanwhile detachments of Black

120

cavalry have pushed up around the flank
of Antony's main force and threaten encirclement,
or to drive the raiders into the Susquehanna
River, which here bursts through the hills in a gorge.
Leaving the Rose and the Lily to engage the main
force of the enemy, Antony wheels and throws
his whole force at the flankers, who are caught by surprise
and scattered. Turning again, he takes the enemy
on their right flank before they recover
from the last charge of the suicide company. But now
massive reinforcements arrive from the city: pretending
that this was not what he expected, Antony
fakes the retreat. Only fifteen riders
of three hundred and sixty of the Rose and Lily
return; and Gareth and Eleanor Madison never
come back to their farm in the broad valley of the Scioto.
And now all Harrisburg empties itself
of armies which join the pursuit of the force of the Spear.
On the Fredericksburg road Jago has arranged a diversion:
a battalion of partisans and Tuscarawan irregulars
wait in ambush where the road passes through woods,
and after a rocket barrage, descends on the Black
Countian armies. There's a brief skirmish, but soon
they break off; this exercise intended
to serve two functions: to give the force
of the Spear time to retreat, and to lull the enemy
into believing the Free Countian trap
has been sprung and what follows is simply a rout.
But the partisans melt into the woods
and close in behind the Messiah's forces
as Antony wheels north, drawing them on
to Manada Gap where the Blue Ridge is pierced
by a valley and a narrow road winds through.
High are the hills and dark are the defiles.
Evening comes on like fate above the pines;
at the mouth of the vale waits the one-eyed man,
his warriors, who have stood in arms all day,
while others fought, split into two brigades
one on each side, ready to go to battle.
The force of the Spear rides forth from the mountain;

they spur their horses, cross the marshy creek,
wheel, and await their enemy. Who now,
seeing their prey at bay before them, form
a line of battle and prepare to charge.
There is a horn blast in the hills and vales:
The army of the Bee's about to sting.
Full on the enemy's flanks and rear they fall:
and as they charge they all begin to sing.
The Black commanders order a retreat,
but foresters and partisans have blocked
the road with fallen trees; their laser beams
command a swathe of open ground. One course
remains: to brush aside the exhausted men
that they've pursued all day, and gain the slope
that faces them, and turn and fight. They still
outnumber their opponents two to one.
But when they reach the brook, the Spear attacks
and charges them as they negotiate
the marshy ground: the Bee, meanwhile, has grouped
and lays a barrage down from either flank
of rockets and of laser fire: behind
the partisans press forward for the kill.
Slowly the summer evening fills the valley
and one by one the hosts of the Jihad
lay down their arms and in their terror beg
forgiveness of the Lord and mercy from
His enemies whom He has given such power.

◆

But Simon has foreseen much that has befallen, and kept
in the city of Carlisle the forces Antony had assumed
had been sent to counter the Tuscarawan invasion.
With these he has followed the pursuit and now is riding
swiftly along the vale to the relief of his armies.
On the field of battle Jago is struck with doubt;
his sword declines; some warrior's sense
or something of the diviner's gift of reading the world
as signs, has given him urgent warning. Gathering
his own guard, some of them Lithend men,
he breaks off from battle, turns, and gallops away,

knowing he will meet his great enemy in the vale.
And so it is. As the light begins to fade
he smites the advance guard of the Messiah's army
and with twenty men left, spurs for the black banner
bearing the device of the raven, where Simon rides
among the picked men of his guard. Jago
seems invulnerable; slaying three men he breaks
the divine circle and comes face to face with his enemy.
Simon calmly dismounts and draws his sword.
Jago does likewise. Meanwhile the Mohican army,
alerted by Jago's assault to the new danger,
has used the time that Jago's sacrifice has given
to confirm their victory, take their prisoners, leave
a rearguard of foresters behind in the woods, and covered
by gathering darkness, slip away to the hills.

◆

Now James is alone in a circle of alien warriors:
in the half-light his eye cannot measure the depth
of the world about him; he is tired, tired, by loss,
grief, long labor, humiliation, anxious
concern for his unborn son, and the unending pain
of his wife's crippling, and his own unintended guilt.
But as a spider, whose web lies in the path
of an officious housemaid's duster, though starved and frail,
remakes every day a web whose beauty and symmetry
diminish each time and decay; till at last a few
tattered and ghastly strands, anchored in a knot,
a hideous shred, hang from the beam; still,
drawing out of herself the torn silk of her existence
the spinner yet renews her work of weaving;
or as the tree whose first buds were broken
in March by a frost, and fall, cased in a jewel
of ice, and whose second budding, still a brave show,
is stricken and snapped by hard winds in April,
nevertheless will put forth a third, stunted
and sickly vesture, easy prey for the beetles
and flies that riot in carnival May; so James
lifts up his head once more, turning from side
to side to catch the lost hemisphere of sight,

and brings his sword into guard, and steadies his arms.
Simon looks at him, and the scar aches in his groin.
He wants this stubborn angelic spirit for his prisoner
and means to exhaust him with meaningless trials of strength.
So he circles to James's left, and strikes; James
spins, parries, ripostes, the sword whooping.
But the jarring counter amazes James with its strength;
his point drops, and Simon strikes for the elbow.
The armor deflects the blow, and James recovers,
but every time he strikes, Simon moves
to the left, and goes out of sight. James tires,
and Simon strikes downward always, making
his enemy spend his power in the parry. In a last
burst of rage, as Simon's sword comes down,
James lunges two-handed at the shoulder joint
and pierces the great muscles of the chest and neck.
Simon's blow shatters his helmet and stuns him,
and both combatants fall apart for a minute.
James gasps, and speaks. "What did you mean
when you called me brother at our last meeting?"
Simon sees his moment, and releases at last
the lie he has long prepared. "You and I
are sons of the same father: Shaker McCloud.
He raped Mary your mother, and she, being a slave
to the cruelty of passion, loved him and cleaved to him. Your wife
is your sister, fool, and your father is not your father:
he whom I slew, whom you loved as a father, debauched
your mother, and being indeed your father, disinherited
you of the lands that your stepfather left you. You owe
me thanks for avenging your griefs on our father: Come
then, and be my second, and you shall share
in the glory of the Jihad and sit at the right hand
of the Messiah." So all is lost: the last wave
of exhaustion breaks over the head of the hero. And, strange,
he remembers a morning in spring on Lithend Farm
when a boy came over to play, and now he recalls
that boy was Simon McCloud; and what a good
time they had, diverting a stream and making
a paddle wheel turn in the current; and how they fought
for control of the best plots in that small Eden;

and Simon, the elder, had got the upper hand,
and in desperation James had bitten his enemy
deep in the shoulder, and tasted the boy-smell and blood;
and how Simon concealed from their parents the fact
of his playmate's guilt, and saved him from punishment; and how
in the battle of St. Clair, Simon and James had fought
shoulder to shoulder against the enemy. And seeing
Simon now, his crazed eyes and tormented
spirit, James pities him, and cannot hate him;
and since all other causes of action—
wife, father, mother, son, self—
have vanished away, he can do nothing. His sword
drops from his hand, and his knees buckle. Night
has fallen, but the ring of torches burns so bright
that he cannot see the stars. Three of the Guard
catch him before he falls, and take him prisoner.

V

◆◆◆◆◆◆◆◆◆◆◆◆◆◆◆◆◆◆◆◆◆

HEALING

1. The Second Meeting with Kingfish

That night the Messiah's army camps
where it is, sending forth scouts to search for the enemy.
Next day dawns pleasantly; James
finds himself wakened by crimson light
filtering through the fabric of a tent canopy.
He is alone, unarmed, but unbound. Hearing his movements,
a soldier comes in with face averted in respect,
bearing a basket of bread, and fruit, and good
Black County cheeses, and a jugful of milk warm
from the cow. A bell strikes, and the man departs
at once, to perform his morning prayers; failure
to do so is death. James falls to
with surprising appetite, giving thanks to Pan for the humble
desires of the flesh. He has no curiosity and drifts off
to sleep as soon as his breakfast is over. Time
passes; he wakes. Despair, when you live there, is not
unpleasant. Shortly after, the tent flap is raised
and Simon comes in. "You will be pleased to learn,"
he says with a smile, "that your people have made their escape.
A well-laid plan, if you will accept
an enemy's compliment. But I'm afraid it serves my purposes;
I needed a great misfortune to weld my slaves
to myself, and this one will do very well. How
do you feel?" "I feel nothing at all," says James.
"Good. That's the beginning of wisdom. Nothing
is pure like the water that cleanses the sore. I've come,
you see, to instruct you into the secret way
of the Messiah." "Why should you trouble to do that?" asks James.
"Should you not simply dispose of me now, or bring me
back in your triumph to impress your followers?" "I want,"
says Simon, "a friend: someone who's neither a fool
nor a slave, but consents to follow me out of free will."
"I see," says James. "What, then, is this secret
way of the Messiah?" "Do not make fun of it, James;
till you know what your wisdom looks like in comparison."
"Fun was not quite my thought, brother," says James.
"That sounds very much like self-pity,

if you'll forgive me for saying so, James. You're lucky.
Events have so fallen out that you have a shortcut
to knowledge many have fought for and failed to find.
Surely even your priests have told you already
that we have no roots, and those that we seem to have
are our enemies, teaching us falsehood and dangerous comfort."
"Yes, my brother Brother Siddhartha said that,"
says James with a smile. "Or if we have roots they are rooted
in every impurity; incest is every man's mother."
"Very good," says Simon. "Then why so bitter about it?"
"It grieves me to think of this world so good and beautiful,"
says James, "and to know it as just a game or an illusion.
Brother, you have taken me out to the darkness where you live
and shown me behind the moon and the mountains, the trees
and the faces of my friends, the scaffolds and props of their falseness.
What, then, shall I do, who feel in myself
still the pulse of life, who hunger and sleep,
who am bound to this hot packet of energies for a time,
who miss the habit of action, the customary illusion
of will and calculation, the sharp drug of hope?"
"This is the secret:" Simon replies; "hate.
Let us throw down the whole superstructure
of deceit; human meanings, which are a filthy disease
on the face of life; life, which crawls and breeds
from the insentient; matter, which is energy grown fetishistic of itself;
energy, whose waves and repetitions show
a brute optimism of survival that must be cauterized;
even the shapes of space and time which follow
the inertia of mathematics. Let us go back
to the most impossible state of all, nothingness:
that, you will find, is a project that will burn your calories
and keep you quite as active as you wish. The work
is ready and waiting; will you join me in it, James?"

♦

To what a place have I come, your poet, that I confess
I do not know how to go on, though the numbers return
and drive the words on from line to line; if he,
my hero (and I see no way for him), if he cannot

escape, then I have no magical gifts left
out of my store, to give him: they are all given already.
O, I might resolve it all by theology: say
that Simon has spoken only the wisdom of Yahman;
that Pan riots on undiminished
in rick, in flower, in torrent and hill and flame,
driving the world to its red-gold fall,
through the brief intake of breath that is winter, and back
into blazing spring, Easter lilies, candles,
the hot thaw that blows up from the Gulf,
the ice riddled and honeycombed, floods like a flash
over the turbid fertile townlands, birdsong;
that the truth of the young girl dying of cancer
is no more true than the truth of the girl
in love with a wonderful guy. Or, friends, I might
in my grief turn to the bright-eyed one, sweet Sperimenh,
dancing in twilight on the scaffolding of the world, soft
breast and smile of a mother, making by magic
the world still come into beauty, into being;
and find by her inspiration a clever device,
a witty machine to rescue my plot, my hero.
But Sperimenh stands aloof, buffing her fingernails:
She's a fair-weather god, as all gods are,
and no blame to her. Theology is no assistance,
and nor, I find now, are the secret powers
of my own being; one not given
to complaint, my misfortunes would not impress a stranger,
but nevertheless at the center of my life I have died.
Well, then, what actually happened
there in the tent on the field of battle, on the day
after the battle, in that valley clad with pines?
What did James do? I'll tell you, dear friends.
He laughed. And at once a vision arose in his mind
of an old black man in a cave long ago.
And Simon, misunderstanding, thinks that James
has given assent to his words and is laughing in ridicule
against the world, and is turned to Simon's purposes;
but James has come out in quite another place.

♦

Simon leaves orders that James be given the run
of the camp, but kept from weapons or horses. That evening
James visits the soldier guarding his arms, on the pretext
of wishing to see if his helmet can still be repaired.
He falls into conversation with the man, and inquires
after the sword Adamant. The soldier takes it
from the great leather case where the armor is stored
and holds it up for James to see. It's another
beautiful evening, the blade glimmers red
along both its surfaces. "Go on, swing it," says James.
"You'll see what I mean: it knows what you want to do."
The young fellow obeys, and the sword whines
in an arc about his head. James hums
under his breath: the sword's mind understands
and suddenly it is as if the weapon had struck
on the massive limb of a tree, for it drops like lead
and strikes, flatlong, the back of the soldier's neck.
Stunned, he falls like a slaughtered ox, though the blow
will leave him with only a headache tomorrow. James
makes sure that no one has seen; donning the cloak
and the helm of the fallen man he binds on his sword
and carrying with him the case of his armor he saunters
idly toward the pickets. A low whistle
and an answering whinny identify grey Gringolet
who stamps with pleasure at seeing his master again.
James strokes the beautiful pewter coat flecked
with silver and delicate touches of charcoal, and holds
for a moment the long sensitive head with its elegant
nostrils, its great wild trusting eye.
Gringolet dances a little, his winglike female
hocks catching the highlights, his skin mobile
over vein and muscle and rocklike bone. Love
for this animal flowers in James' heart, and he throws
the case of armor over his neck, and vaults
silently onto his back. The sentry approaches
but seeing the uniform of the Black Guard
he nods, thinking the man has been sent by the Messiah
to give the magnificent beast an hour of exercise.
They are not challenged until the edge of the camp;
James tightens his knees and the horse collects

itself like a wave and springs forward, almost
leaving the man on his back behind. His hooves
batter the turf, and the wind dashes his mane
like a flag against the bloody nose of his rider;
a barrier of logs marks the camp's boundary
but Gringolet scarcely lengthens his stride, and soars
over, his hooves trailing, vanishes in the dark.
Pursuit is useless; no animal on earth
can match the mount of Shaker McCloud, of the hero
who bears the sword of George Quincy of Lithend.

◆

And under the stars, blue Vega in Lyra,
mighty Hercules with his red head, Deneb
scorching in the Northern Cross, Altair in Aquila,
James sets his back to Arcturus the Watcher and rides
for Pegasus rising now in the eastern sky.
He has one aim for the moment: to find Kingfish
and learn once and for all the truth of his birth;
the great pictures we have put in the sky guide him
east toward Hattan and the light of the rising sun.

◆

In two days he has gained the Hattan Burbs
and on the third he breaks the undergates
and stands once more in the presence of the strange old man.
"What for you bother pore ole Kingfish
wid' his achin' ass an' mo' years den a turkle?"
"I come to ask a question, since, in the past
you gave me help and answers when I needed them. Do so
again, and I will promise any gift
in exchange, that you desire and I command."
Kingfish's face brightens. "A question you got for me,
son? What be your question?" "This," says James.
"Who was my father?" Kingfish saddens. "Dey never
thinks to ask. Pore achin' ass.
The answer to dat ain't no surprise: yo' father
was George Quincy, jus' like ah said." "So Simon
lied!" cries James, astonished by this simplicity.
"Then who was my mother?" "Mary his wife. Boy,

133

yo' ask the dumbest questions ah ever hear."
"Then why did Simon call me his brother?" "Cause dat's
what he be," says Kingfish complacently. "So my father—" says James.
"Were de lover ob Simon's mother," says Kingfish, "What
were her name now? Emily McCloud, ah think de man say.
Look, son, why yo' puzzle yo' haid
wid all dese questions? Don't make no difference,
de moment yo' got enough troubles to ask de questions,
what de answer might be. De doubt don't
go away if yo' git de answer yo' want. De doubt
jus' burrow deeper, like an ol' crayfish
in de mud, like piss in de snow. Yo' done
broke through de doors ob de edge ob de world
an' now yo' want to know how yo' can love
what yo' seen from outside. Ah got a question for you:
Why not? Ain't dat a sucker?" "If the world is a game,"
says James, "knowing that, how can I act
with all the pitch and momentum of action, if life
is merely illusion? Should I not rather shut
myself up in contemplation, and be as the Brahmins?"
"Come here, boy," says Kingfish. "Closer."
The old man suddenly raises his stick
and strikes James sharply over the head.
"What did you do that for?" James asks angrily.
"Dat hurt, don' it?" says the old man.
James nods. "Well dat was a game. Who
gonna tell you a game ain't anything less dan life?
Love de game, boy: de flesh be de life
ob de spirit, an' de spirit be all a game. But de game
be all dat dere be, boy, an' dat be better
dan nothing." "But if I am to play the game that is given me,"
James cries in despair, "then it is my duty
to kill the brother I loved, once, when we played
together as boys on the farm; and if all men
are my brothers, since incest is our condition, then I must slay
whole holocausts of kin, as if their lives
were nothing; and being already a great slayer
of men, my arms are bloody, I am weary of war
and the sight of death, and the life that feeds upon death.
What sacrifice will suffice to purify me and purge

134

my deeds of the blood that is on them?" "De sacrifice, boy,
be yo' life itself. If yo' feel de guilt ob de game
de guilt pays for de guilt. Contemplation
for you be de life ob duty." "But might I not,"
says James in a sigh of fear and grief, "be a monster,
so certain that some crime is my duty that I
become not a human being, but some terrible
filthy angel of blood? How, if I play
the game as you ask, am I distinguished from Simon?"
"Yo' plumb forget what ah tol' you, boy. If yo'
turn back to de worl' dat yo left, and love de pore
sweet rag of a thing dat it be, den you
be engaged, no shit, to believe in de goods
dat it sets up for you; justice, and mercy, and love,
and de holy spirit. Dey ain't gone away for you
jus' 'cause Simon done turn away from dem:
ah ain't sayin' it's easy, boy; believin'
de way dat yo' do, yo' a whole lot stronger
dan other men, except for rascals like Simon; yo' in
a position to do a whole lot ob harm if yo' make
a single mistake, boy, an' dat is yo' problem."
"But how can I kill if the good is based upon life?"
"Dat's where yo' wrong. Life is based on de good."
"But who decides what is the good?" "All ob us."
"Even the hosts of the Messiah?" "Yes, boy,
even dem: but de way dey choose to cast
dey vote be by death and killing: respeck dem, boy,
and use de kind of vote dat dey use
when yo' deals wid dem." This time, without let or obstacle,
James bursts into laughter. "Who would have thought it
so simple, after all? Kingfish, show me yourself
as you are, that I may remember your words and never
forget the joy of my grief and the great grief
of my joy." "Yo' quite sure, boy, dat yo' want
to see ol' Kingfish widout his false teeth,
an' widout his ol' black skin, an' widout
his achin' bones? Den watch, boy, and speak
if yo' cain't bear it no mo'." Now it seems to James
that Kingfish explodes in a billion faces, mouths,
arms, and terrible eyes. Thunder crashes;

the walls of the cave disappear, and fires, burning
on fires, blossom about them; the floor disappears
and suddenly Kingfish spreads and becomes a thousand
tongues of molten being reaching out
from the face of the world sphere; the dance of the tongues
is like maidens who dance in a meadow, and now Kingfish
is one only, a girl in a green silk dress
holding a child and a mirror, bright as the sun
and simple as springtime. At this last vision
James is so afraid that he calls out,
and at once the dear familiar face of the old
man is before him again, as clear and open
as a vessel of water drawn from a running spring.

◆

In the following days Kingfish and James work
at the laser forges, annealing the cloven helm
and bonding the golden ginkgo leaf, which Simon's
blow had shorn off, to the glittering surface. And then
Kingfish makes James lie down and puts him to sleep;
and when he awakes Kingfish has disappeared,
but the Guardian Angels whose office it is to attend him
insist that James wait in the caves, to receive
a great gift that Kingfish is now preparing.
A week later James is again cast
into sleep, and it seems in a dream that his brain has been split
and only the small, dry, rational world
of the left has been open to waking awareness; the right
with its glows and gulfs, its great aching melodies,
its swift summations, in mysterious shapes, of multitudes,
has been closed: but now, in cascades, the right world
comes crashing in like an unknown ocean, the schism
is healed, and the whole universe springs into depth
and time. He wakes, and his head aches. It seems
to him as if somehow a screen of raspy sounds
had been set over his consciousness; yet it tickles pleasantly
and is not inconsistent with color and form, though its fringes
have much the taste of a smell or of heat and cold.
Kingfish has set in the blind socket a new
miraculous eye, with its own brain, and spliced

136

its output not only across the chiasmus to the visual
cortex but also into the olfactory bulb,
with a bleed into the midbrain, and a feedback loop
through the auditory cortices on both sides of the brain.
More information than from any natural eye
will pour from this organ: it perceives far beyond
the narrow window of visible wavelengths, far
beyond the infrared and the ultraviolet.
The surplus processing power of much of the brain
must be called in to take up the additional load
and James must learn like a baby to use his new eye.
At first that screen interferes with familiar sight:
but a strange analogy makes itself felt; with an effort
like that by which we resolve the two ghostly
images of an object close to the eyes into one,
he begins to recover the depth and roundness that we
and a few of our sister species have given the world.
But now he sees, as it were, a fringe of color
not blazing outside the objects he sees
but strangely, glowing inside them: colors that are
to violet as violet's is to blue, and to red as red
is to yellow. They taste hotter and finer on one
side, and softer and duller on the other, than colors
he's ever seen before. And soon those colors
begin to form shapes, that are sharper on one side, and heavier,
thicker and slower on the other: he sees the air
roil and crawl over a heated surface,
the flush under the skin of his attendants where arteries
warm the surface: even the specters of bones
behind the flesh. The dark disappears, for everything
glows and fluoresces before him: he must learn to sleep.

◆

James renews his offer of any service
or gift it is in his power to give in return;
but Kingfish puts him off, complains of his "achin'
ass," and shuffles away. At last, on the day
that James has fixed to take his departure, Kingfish
replies: "Jus' visit dis ol' man
one more time again. And dis time

think to ask de question and remember, trouble
come to every man and each can help
his neighbor better sometime dan he can hisself."

2. Adventures

"So what happened next?" says Ruth, sleepily, settling
the baby softly to suck at her breast. "No,"
says James, "you tell me what happened to you."
"I will, but first you must finish your story," says Ruth.

♦

"On good advice I took the northern route:
a flatboat up the Hudson in the fall
where miles of lazy light shone from the river
and bluffs with castles on them, guarding vines
turned upside down upon the mirror surface.
Then westward overland to Watertown
on Lake Ontario, where I had hopes
an Edsel agency or office might
be found, to book a passage through the Lakes
to harbor at Sandusky, and get home
without alerting spies of my return.
I found the warehouse quarter and the docks
in turmoil with the military trade;
a little girl I met directed me
to where the Edsel factor had his chandler's.
I booked a passage for my horse and me
upon a cargo ship that would depart
tomorrow, and I found a quiet inn.
I'd tried to get a sunplane earlier:
but all the planes were requisitioned for
the war, and all the airstrips watched by spies.
The ship was slow but seaworthy: two sails
guided by mikes, like pylons, turned to catch
the wind. We had an uneventful passage
tacking for three calm days across the lake

until we sighted land—the long dark ridge
whose scarp is cut by the Niagara Falls.
In Bufflo Riot I took another ship
and at the captain's table, to my surprise
and great delight, Skip Edsel was my host.
He'd heard of my arrival and had sailed
at once from Cedar Point to meet me here
blown by a following wind. We dined on salmon
caught by the Canuck fisherman up north
and killed a bottle of Les Tres Riches Heures.
But on the morrow it dawned red and wild
and soon there struck a dreadful autumn storm.
The short waves of the lake reared up like hands;
a lace of foam smeared on their fresh grey faces;
the men put out a sea-anchor that held
only an hour or two, and then we drifted;
lightning and thunder split from the old war
between the southern airmass and the arctic;
all night we fought to keep her head upwind
and in the morning light the gale died down
and there before us was a rocky isle.
'I'd know that island anywhere,' said Skip.
'If that's not Pelee, I'm a salted alewife.
We're almost home, my lads. The storm turned round
and drove us on our way. Pan's balls, our luck
has held. Steer south for Put-in-Bay, my boys.'
Skip, as you see, has mastered quite the tang
of sounding nautical. But round the point
appeared another vessel, swift and low
and from its tops there burst the scarlet wolf
betokening the pirates of Lake Huron,
fierce Scottish Canucks dwelling on the bays
of Manitoulin Island, where they prey
on merchant shipping plying in the lakes.
They grappled, boarded, but I led some men
in a charge that scattered the enemy;
I boarded them, hoping to take their ship
and give it as a prize to Skip, who'd shown
such kindness to me always, but they cut
the ropes that bound the ships, and sailed away.

Seeing myself surrounded, I gave in;
I had no armor, and they carried lasers.
They dealt, I have to say, quite kindly with me:
though I could barely understand their speech
they told me I'd be carried back alive
to hear the judgment of the pirate Laird
Red Rory McNeill, Master of the Isle;
this was their furthest southern cruise, and last
before the winter season; they had bribed
the matriarchs of Detriot Riot to let
them through the passage of St. Clair; and now
returned, laden with booty from the South.
They bound me as we sailed through the straits,
but when the water changed to winey blue,
blazing with light as if the depths were lit
by some electric element or dye,
denoting that we swam in northern waters,
they set me free, but watched me carefully.
Those late fall days were deeply beautiful:
the little islands, clad with birches, blazed;
the fine ship swept and lifted with the breeze
under the three tall pylons of her sails;
and soon we raised the piney slopes and roofs
of Michael's Bay, and tied up at the wharves.
They took me to a handsome wooden house
and locked me in a room without a window.
Still, I was well attended: a pretty girl
brought me a meal of trout and applesauce
and talked to me, and let me know my trial
should be three days hence, when her father came
from hunting on Fitzwilliam Island; that
her father was no less than Rory McNeill.
The trial—" "Stop right there," Ruth interrupts.
"Tell me some more about this girl. She saved
your life, I'll bet, and what I want to know
is what she got for payment; also how
she looked, and what you talked about." "If, love,"
says James, "you'll tell me straight away about
the birth and doings of our baby boy."
"You've got a deal," she says. "The girl," says James,

140

"was named Vaille, a Scottish name, though how
they spelled it there I do not know. She was
eighteen, and beautiful." "More beautiful
than me?" asks Ruth. "Oh, certainly," says James.
"Then why did you come back?" "I missed the farm,"
says James. "Poor baby," Ruth sings to the boy,
"you've got a faithless father with a heart
of stone, to cruelly treat poor maidens so."
"Her hair," says James as if she had not spoken,
"was finest blonde, like silk. Her skin was white
and clear without a single freckle—" ("Snake!"
says Ruth, who freckles easily) "—her figure slim
but softly rounded like a pigeon or
a foal, her lips like coral, sea-blue eyes.
This nymph was a warm-blooded creature of
the icy northern seas—" "Don't overdo it,"
Ruth interrupts, "You'll strain credulity."
"In any case," says James, "we hit it off,
and I, to save its life, bring back to you
a body that has been on loan to one
who used it gently and who renders it
undamaged to its true and lovely queen."
"Spoken most gallantly; the hypocrite
has paid his little debt to virtue with
a handful of fine words. The trial, then:
she pled for you, and so they let you live?
A story so well-worn it must be true:
guilt would concoct a fresher cover tale."
"Madam," says James with dignity, "I yield
myself to whatsoever savage justice
you propose, so you will tell me how
our son was born, and what his life has been."

◆

"Listen," says Ruth, suddenly serious,
"You are the one who broods on the nature of value,
though for you it's the value of action, not knowledge, you question;
help me with this if you can, and be my friend.
When my time drew near, Mary your mother came to me
and nursed and comforted me with hardly a word.

I don't fully understand her, James, but I learned
new things from her that I must try to fit
with all that I know. This giving birth, for instance:
I worked for years to know the history, science,
and law of Mohican County: one day,
I know, I shall rule it as Praetor—well, I think;
and giving birth is just a series of spasms
spawned by the autonomous nervous system, assisted
or thwarted by conscious preparations; but it seems to me
I've learned something important, though I know not what.
It has something to do with the fact that the flesh is the spirit's
utterance, its actuality here in the world:
I wove that child there in my womb
though I knew not that I was doing the weaving;
and what, then, is doing, or knowing, or 'I,'
if without will I should know to do what I never
through study or practice knew how to do? I thought
I should solve it by saying that I am not my body;
but that is simply untrue; if I am anything,
James, I am what I was when the baby came,
and that was a body, that can jettison organs as great
and heavy in pounds as the placenta; and yet, if you've seen
a placenta, it looks like a thing you find on a slab
at the butcher's, down in the covered market on Gay Street.
But it's a noble organ, a great piece of the spirit
nevertheless. We are much more, my love,
than what we can take credit for. Biology may not be destiny
but my body is myself, and bodies are the last gift
of all the ages of the past. And we have passed
the gift along. Look at him: isn't he beautiful?
He's like the present as it really is, not as we hold it
by convention: he's hardly human, but absolutely
yet already a person: he's not a being but a striving
to be, as the present is, and that's the only time we are.
Everything we are is a giving away, a greeting,
a goodbye. I baptized him Daniel, as we agreed,
after my father's given name. He was conceived
the night before Shaker died. But please go on
with your tale: how long did you stay with the pirates?"

◆

"I was part-prisoner upon the island,
but Rory took to me and kept me by him;
we would go fishing on the ice, and hunt
the bear and wolf upon the snowy isles,
and come at evening to the hall, where Vaille
served us with roasts and heady honey wine.
They were a patriarchal tribe, and gave
their daughters just as if a human being
might by an alchemy become possessed
of another; as if a person might
be precious for another reason than
their occupation by a self. It's strange
how savage customs have a beauty sometimes:
could Helen be as beautiful if she
were all responsible for what she was?
Vaille was to me, as you must know, my love,
the first woman that I had ever pleased
in the sweet humility of human flesh.
In spring the pirates launched their wooden ships
the day the pack-ice melted; I had begged
permission from Red Rory to embark
with him, and cruise the dark blue waves
of Lake Superior. Vaille wept and watched
the brave ship out to sea. There, as you know,
the great dirigibles of your brother's fleet
painted in yellow, with insignia
of scarlet, brown, and gold, discovered us—
the westernmost of seven fleets you sent
to seek the errant carcass of your lover.
The fight was long and fierce; I climbed aboard
the galleon *Montgolfier*, but as
we broke away the lasers of the *Wolf*,
Red Rory's ship, raked us from stem to stern;
the helium foam was scarcely scorched, but both
the engines jammed and three gondolas, cut
from their moorings, fell away; the great craft
soared out of control into the blue air.
I was alone with no recourse; the airship rose
sounding toward the sun, and headed south.
All I could do was wait until the fuel

was burned, or loss of gas should drop the ship
where I might risk a leap to solid ground.
All day and through the night the engines droned.
I passed, I know, that night, over the fields
of our Mohican County as it slept:
I cried to be where you might be, and yearned
for the strings of lights, like golden bubbles
lacing the bosom of the sleeping land.
At dawn the airship dropped and mountains rose;
a long ridge of azure now barred the way;
the engines failed and fell to silence; soon
with the breeze that strangely I did not feel
the craft was skimming treetops, rose and fell
above a land I did not know, so lush
and purple-green it seemed a paradise.
We scraped upon the ridge and there before me
the land fell off away to distant hills.
I seized my chance, and jumped; alone I stood
in a new world, upon its highest roof.
An anxious farmer with a laser-gun
had seen the strange encounter of the ship
and the mountain, and took me prisoner.
This place was Blue Ridge County, so he said;
his accent and his skin were soft and brown.
I'd landed, then, within the ancient state
of Jorgia where the southern spring
had almost turned to summer in the sun.
He took me to the high court of the queen
of Blue Ridge County: she was tall and black
and wore a blue mantle beautifully:
that was a happy place, gardens so rich
they fed all appetites of flesh and soul;
their dances and their sweet philosophy
entranced me so that if I had not felt
in my memory all that pain and grief
burned like a scar upon the innocence
of flesh, I might have stayed forever there,
yielding at last to that queen's soft desire
and ruling as her consort in a land
that flowed with milk and seldom knew the cold.

144

Her purpose being gently put aside
she nursed a jealousy within her heart
and would not let me go. At last, in haste
and desperation I suborned the mate
of a trading starship, and stowed away,
hoping to have them set me down at once
on old Mount Verdant Field; the Captain, though,
was angry, and refused. I worked my passage
out to the 'Gellan worlds, and worked it back;
I shall not speak of those so many worlds
so various and strange and lovely in
the sky. I stood, at last, upon a golden
hill in Calyforny and waved goodbye
to all my shipmates; found my way to 'Frisco,
banged on the western office of the House
of Westinghouse, and got a message through
to Doug McCloud, who sent a sunplane for me.
I was asleep when we bumped down, as you,
my darlings, are; it was too long a tale."

3. The Joy of Love

"I'm not asleep," Ruth answers sleepily.
"But you must tell me why you did not come
at once to see me, after two whole years,
and why you made a secret of return."
"Two reasons, love. I knew from Doug that you
believed me dead upon the stricken airship
and since my life might be a burden to you
I fixed with myself that I should find out
how all things stood with you, and if
you had, perhaps, with Antony or some
persistent lover, formed a family
to keep yourself and our boy baby warm,
then I should pass away and in disguise
slay or attempt to slay the wretched Simon,
release him from the life he loathed and scourged.

145

The other reason showed itself at once.
Our war was going badly: Antony
had as you know escaped with all his force
from the blind clutches of the Black Jihad;
but in the rearguard action at the fords
was wounded badly and must yield command
to lesser generals. Our spirits flagged,
our arms were weary: both the commanders gone,
and the Mad armies swarming the frontiers;
there was no time to save the wreck of home,
for the great wave of the Messiah's host
was climbing the horizon of the east.
I know that you had nursed poor Antony
and heard from Billy Blubaugh that you sought
a marriage with him and had gained consent
from family and county for the match:
half mad with grief I rode for the frontier
armored and horsed as of old, and resolved
to die in victory. But you have heard
how my coming lifted the hearts of those
that followed me, and how the Black Jihad
quailed when they saw my banners, in the dawn,
blazing with ginkgo leaves, the sign of death,
break from the standards of besieged Ahiah,
and how we burst upon them by surprise
and drove them from the field, and how at last
I smote my brother Simon and cast him down.
I pitied him, I fear, and let him go:
he shall not trouble us again unless
the will of Yahman seeks our utter ruin."
"But how did you, the bridegroom, come to me
that night when all the candles burned and I
awaited my old lover in the dark?"
"Swiftly I rode (the cables being cut)
to bring the good news to Mohican County.
Our victory had not preceded us
and in the night I came to where you lay
and saw our baby Daniel sleeping in
his little bed: I knew that he was mine
and never in my life could I give up

146

that sweet warm breath, that leaf and subtle feather.
I sought out Antony and found him up,
scarcely recovered from his deep head-wound
but all prepared to make his tryst with you.
When he saw me, almost he broke his heart:
that night you had lit candles in the window,
awaited his expected coming in.
Antony raged against me and we fought:
I was the stronger, being unwounded; we
sank in each other's arms for grief and love
(for we, as men do who fight back to back
had learned to love each other in those battles),
and might not do each other harm, being pained
more by the other's grief than by our own,
and Antony in all his shame and sorrow
found a strange joy in my despaired return.
He gave me all his share in you, and in
the greatness of his heart he vowed his fealty
to me in all the years to come, and gave
in the ecstasy of generosity
the keys and deeds to me of Lithend Farm,
my father's home and now at last my own.
I clothed myself in Antony's best clothes
and shaved my head, like his, and bandaged it
as if I bore his wound upon my brow,
and darkened all my white skin with a salve,
and came to you at night as if I were
your lover. But you, like a tired bird,
had fallen asleep upon your silks and furs
naked, but for a fold of lace that fell
across your thighs, and for your hair
that covered up your breasts like waves of fire
in the candlelight. I put out the candle;
your body glowed as if its vital heat
were incandescent, for my eyes were magic
and knew the courses of your blood within
the sacred whiteness of your queenly flesh.
And in the dark you woke, and groaned, and asked
why I had been so late, and in a whisper
I replied: something about the dressing

147

of my wound. You had a bowl of fruit
and offered it: I smelled the dented pears,
the fragrant tangerines, the milky musk
of cantaloupes, but put the vessel by
and laid my hand upon your belly and
sighed, and kissed. But I must know, my love,
when was it that you knew your lover for
himself, and gave yourself to me, not him?"
Ruth shifts sleepily in her nest of down.
"At once in my body, but not at once
in my mind. But it was as if the curse
had been removed, and I was in a dream
where frozen flesh may speak, and gates that have
been shut for many years may open and
give upon gardens wet with morning dew;
and where a person may be two, like twins,
and where two friends may be rolled into one."
James presses his questions: "Ruth, were you angry
at learning how you'd been deceived, or how
light-minded I can be when desperate,
playing so trivial a trick upon
my friend and lover? I have learned to laugh,
my darling, when the pains of life are greatest,
and play by any rules that serve the time:
but it would tear my heart in two if you
took it as meaning any disrespect
for you, or holding of you cheap." Ruth speaks:
"No, what I felt was sheer astonishment,
much the same sweet bewilderment
as when our baby swam into the world:
and all the freshness of this life, so wild
and full of springs and mornings, broke on me;
blank admiration for your presumption
and resolve, and pity for Antony.
It was as if my self had burst into
a thousand fragments, and a rainbow only
hung where the fixed world had been; but I
was more myself than ever I was before.
But what was it for you, my crazy heart?"
"Solemn and lovely, like a Christmas carol:

It was a stem of Jesse sang in me
and you, my smudged Madonna, were the crib
where I laid me down beneath the star.
Holy and sweet, but like the clowns that tumble
when the circus comes to town. I can't say
how it was: to speak of it, it would be
desecrated if it were not so strong
or funny: yet I love to speak of it."
"And it's bad luck," says Ruth, "to speak of it.
So why do I, almost asleep with my
baby, most soft to all the terrible storms
that life can send, not care a fig for luck?"
"I think," says James, "that in the pride of joy
we thumb our noses at the dark event:
a joy which must go muffled and in secret
is not so full as not to doubt itself.
Nothing can take, my love, this moment from us:
it will go flying out forever to the ends
of the universe undying: the gods
have their impossible nuptials in our room,
and words, which fix and catch, have gone all mad
and they themselves make midnight carnival
and couple in the forest of the signs,
knowing each other and themselves so wildly
that all their clutching turns to fire and life,
and freedom blossoms from the tree of tongues."
"And some would say," Ruth answers merrily,
"that anyone as eloquent as you,
my love, has half his mind on nouns and verbs
and half upon his own sweet sentiments
and none left for his lover. Heroes are,
alas, notoriously prone to words:
but I'll forgive you for your blue blue eyes
though one of them, I know, is fake." James, caught,
recovers quickly. "Madam, it is you
who've talked your pretty white ass out of trouble:
I come home and I find my wife preparing
for a lover; no Penelope she;
I see the headlines in the *Verdant Star*:
'Cuckolded General Slays Wife: Judge Sets

The Minimum Sentence: "Suffered Enough"
Defense Attorney Says.' " Ruth is as quick:
"I should have cut your windpipe in your bath,
you bully, with your tales of pirate girls.
The male, I think, has his balls in his head
and all his brains are in his precious balls.
Don't wake the baby, you barbarian."

4. The Garden

After the defeat of the Black Countian armies
and the rout that followed, and the truce that threw the Jihad
back over the Ahiah River, the absence
of the Messiah grows into the main grief of his hosts:
his generals sign the protocols in his absence, the elders
confirm them; but neither on the field of battle where the search
by his grieving disciples is permitted as part of the terms
of their surrender, nor in the accustomed dwellings of the Messiah
may he be found, alive or dead; it is
as if he'd been taken to Heaven by his angels, or perhaps,
as some of the more ambitious Elders are whispering,
down into Hell. But Simon is neither in Heaven
nor Hell; after his casting down by his brother
he has covered himself with a cloak and slipped away,
reaching his tents in secret and rousing a servant,
the one who loves him the most; with the help of this man
he disguises himself as a back-country landowning
knight of the army of Susquehanna: the servant
saddles a horse for his master and, at his command,
kneels before him bowing his head for the stroke.
Simon slays the fellow lest weakness or drink
betray the secret intentions of his divine master
to his lieutenants and followers, and at once takes his departure,
galloping east and north in the gathering dusk.
It is in his mind that he must go to the mountain
and wait for a certain term of years till his followers
find that they cannot survive without him, and pray

for his return; and he needs some conference with the dark forces
he serves; so he makes his way to Mount Katahdin
in the old North County of Maine, and dwells
naked in a cave by a well, and is fed like a holy man
by the dour farmers of the region, upon milk and grain.

◆

But for ten years Mohican County bathes
in the golden sunlight of peace and heavenly plenty;
they are the years of Daniel Quincy's boyhood
as he grows from a baby fat and pink as a peach
to a one-toothed goofy small gnome
to a gurgling toddler beating the air with his hands
to a bright little chatterbox running up and downstairs,
his heels thumping on the oak floors of the farm
at Lithend, his room ghastly with frogs and beetles,
his ways watchfully guarded by McArgus the dog
who has carefully marked out the whole territory
where the boy roams, with warning dribbles of virulent
male pee. Ruth and James live half
of the year at Wolverton Hill, and half at Lithend;
being of great estate, they take on partners
who act as bailiffs, laborers, craftsmen, vintners,
move in with their families and work the bounteous soil.
Spring in Ahiah begins with the roar of the floods
carrying baulks of ice maneuvering clumsily
down past the rapids, and spreading silently over
the fields; the sheltered dells show brilliant patches
of green, and watercress multiplies in marshy ground;
in the woods the snowdrops cluster and dangle, the crocuses'
butter or yolk or egg-blue or imperial
shadowy purple or star-throated or sky
comfort the gnarled feet of the oaks; daffodils
burst, and aconite, ranged panicles of creamy
snowball viburnum, deep green grass,
lawns purple with violets, the forests lit
to their floors by the mild nuptial light of April
(by June they'll be dark as a green cave).
The rivers run clear at last and turn blue; the first
hot day, hot as a steambath, comes

after Easter with its bells, water, candles, and incense;
the air fills with the delicate stink of the apple
blossom, the cherry, gigantic mounds of lavender
tree-wisteria, peonies crimson and white,
the irises bearded, indigo, bronze, or pink
or, later, white, precise, Siberian, set
in the damper places by pools with waterlilies.
And summer comes with the first thunderstorm, new
leaves shaking themselves with the blows of the great
drops thrown from the lumbering sky, the streams
yellow with clay, the farmer cursing the hail;
and everything closes in to a green shade,
the lilies explode from their scapes and sway over wilder-
nesses of spears; and now the hours of lassitude
come, the creaking of growing corn and cane,
the wheat so rich the stems taste of green
milk, and the fish fatten, waterlogged, in the streams;
the ripening corn and tomatoes, eggplant and squash
promising wine-hazed afternoons of cooking
and fresh pastas with basil, and grapeleaves stuffed,
and strawberry feasts with cream from the churn and honey
robbed from the hives at Wolverton Hill Farm.
Friends come round with musical instruments, play
all the hot night in the screened-in porches, the babies
in bed, the conversation becoming philosophic;
naked to sleep in the arms of your lover under
the glass dome of the chamber, the glimmering stars.
And then fall, with its quiet fires and bushels of fruit,
the forested land struck orange by magic,
the first lonely days of wind and rain
when the gale blowing around the eaves makes you want
to travel a long way away to a chimney-corner
in foreign parts, and the first plays of the season
open along the marquees on Gay Street;
But then the frost, and twenty successive days
of golden weather, scorching at noon, and the apples
and peaches bulging in monstrous shapes, the sap
so abundant and rich it seems they will burst, and the grapes
in enormous baskets, thrown in the stained winepress.
And so the winter comes, with a warm day

that changes to rain, and a raw chill toward nightfall,
the rain turning to sleet in the night, and by morning
there's four or five inches of snow. But it melts
at once, and one of the last roses blooms
a day or two later; and then the bitter cold
comes down from the north, the sprouts and cabbages
writhe in the kitchen garden, dead birds
can be found frozen by waysides, and the red berries
of dogwood and blackthorn, viburnum, the hips of the briar
offer themselves to the living. Snow falls
upon snow; powdery bombs drop from the trees
and at evening the windless zero glows on pans
and scars of melted and frozen ice; fresh
snow, dyed blue, is lit to orange
by eve's cool bonfire. Christmas carols,
gold Hanukkah candles; the rising of the sun
and the running of the deer, the playing of the merry organ,
sweet singing in the choir. At home, fires roar.
The boy in his pajamas gets drowsy in the heat, is carried
upstairs asleep. And then the bleak days
of Lent, Ahiah like a tundra, pinkish grasses
spiked through the snow, the big straggly hackberry
tree casts a long shadow, brief thaws
that smell of rotted corn; sometimes brown
fields, grey horizons, enormous sky.
And then spring again, as it was before.
Birds singing and the brown spate's roar.

♦

James and Ruth plant a garden up where the bluffs
rise from the river and a cliff of buttery, pinkish
sandstone, cleft by a falling stream, has been cut
by the swing of the meander. A long island a little
downstream, with a foamy prow, is bridged by a pair
of delicate arches laid from the same stone
as the cliff; across the river a marsh with pools
is planted with irises, bulrushes, nenuphars, ferns;
old logs and mounds of dry moss make seats;
the island is planted with tulips, orchises, flowering
cherries, and tree-peonies; the cliff with sedum,

ageratum, heathers and ericas, junipers;
above there's a walled garden with roses and espaliered
pears, and a long walk of carnations, phloxes,
sweet william, delphiniums, allium towering
out of a white haze of baby's breath, speedwell
and primrose edging the border; a square lawn
divided by white gravel paths, centered
upon a formal pond with a Hermes, box
hedges, lavender. A long walk bordered
with golden ginkgos. Where the soil is thin and the sun
shines hotly, a knot garden of herbs
is set, with sage and chervil, burnet and thyme
and basil and anise, lemon balm, mint, coriander;
and further back, beyond a belt of woodland
pierced by grassy walks looking out on the hills
and underplanted with rhododendrons, azaleas,
a kitchen garden is sown in fertile soil
with stone paths and bordered by hedges of lilacs.

◆

And this garden is a garden of time. Over years
the great flowering chestnuts grow, and the willows
across the river in the water garden gather
mass, and the small bonsai pines, on the cliff
and the rock garden, establish definitive oddities;
and every year the flower beds change their beautiful
vesture, yellow to blue to crimson to pink,
the tall madonna lilies and phloxes burst
like starshells or rockets out of the earth; the lawns,
speckled with daisies in spring, become deeper and bluer
in fall. And often the folk of the County by invitation
wander the garden and take slips, or bring
to the gardeners cuttings or seeds of their own.
For gardens walled off entirely from time and the world
will flourish only as gloomy kingdoms of death;
and the Sun, the mine where every delicate leaf
digs its ethereal fuel, is owned in common
by any who knows how to give thanks
by turning the fire to the work of construction; from the long
death of that star, burning the first gas

of the universe, this sweet world of water, poised
between vapor and ice, performs its miraculous play
of creation and fabricates richer gardens of time.

♦

And time passes; by secret messages Simon
calls to himself in Maine his most faithful disciples;
they, in turn, whisper the news that the Messiah's
not dead, but fasts in the wilderness; pilgrims begin
to attend his cave, and marvel, returning to tell
their friends. Simon chooses one man,
the brother of him that he slew when he fled the field
of battle, telling him James Quincy murdered
his brother, and training him in the arts of hate and deception;
and when he is ready, he sends the man to Mohican
with orders to take up service with James,
pretending to love the freedom of Mohican County
and renounce the true belief of his home and his fathers.

♦

In her fifth year as elector, Ruth is voted
a senator. The Whig reaction after the war
left only a few Tories on their seats, but Ruth,
being one of them, led the Tory counterattack
four years later. Ruth and James
are like giants bestriding the world; under their care
the County blossoms and prospers, its arts ripen,
history seems to answer their will and intention.
Two more children are born to them: Adam
and Maia, the sweet apples of married passion.
In the sixth year after the fall of Simon
James in pity takes on as a servant a man
called Judd who claims to have fled from the Black Counties,
a thin, quiet fellow who looks trustworthy:
Judd becomes a favorite of young Daniel
and takes him hunting for deer in the autumn woods.

♦

In the tenth year after James's return Ruth
is named and chosen by the retiring Praetor Elizabeth

as her favored successor; the Senate's vote confirms it;
and now Ruth must prepare to give herself utterly
in the coming fall to the service of Mohican County.
On one of the last days of summer, she and James
take a picnic into their garden, cold chicken,
yeasty and crusty bread, salt butter,
mild Amish cheese, and white wine.
Hot raspberries picked from the loaded canes
are all their dessert, and the wine is cooled in the stream.
They work, or wander together without a word,
or talk of all their past, and the oddness of life,
and the lives of their children, the coming burden of duty;
and in the heat of the afternoon they kiss
in the arbor, and fall asleep for an hour, and wake
as the evening cools and the delicate columns that ring
the small marble Aphrodite are lit from across
the western valley by low rays of the sun.
In the far woods one of the trees has blanched
into crimson, and the blue air is still and quiet.
They fall silent; at last James sighs
and turns to Ruth, and speaks. "It's perfect. No man
deserves such happiness, least of all me. Come
what may in the dark of the future, I say to you
that no one has cause to grieve for me." His eyes, older
now with the fine lines of thirty-six years,
are strangely blue as ever; Ruth frowns.
"What do you mean, my love? I know you've the Sight:
do you foresee some terrible thing in the future?
Or is it rather a fear that I shall neglect you,
being, it makes me laugh to think it, mother
now to my people? If it's the latter, why,
poor boy, you can always go back to *your* mother."
He smiles. "You're droll, as usual, at my expense.
I meant nothing; or if—it was nothing to fear
for we've won, my darling; we've carried away the jackpot
and spent it, and no one can take it back. If ever. . . ."
"Don't speak," says Ruth, and kisses his mouth;
"I know what is in your mind; it's also in mine."

VI

◆◆◆◆◆◆◆◆◆◆◆◆◆◆◆◆◆◆◆

THE SHADOW OF
DEATH

1. Winter

These notes to tragic. Time was the poison
milked from the snake to cure us from death in innocence.
In that sad height of knowing, the kingdoms
beneath us, we are most liable to be cast down.
Light clenched itself into the spring of matter,
matter shuddered into the prurience of life,
life screamed, and gave birth to the terror of death:
that achieved freedom, won by intrinsicate order,
is burst in a moment when a single thread is pulled.

♦

Not with a blowing of trumpets, a glitter of arms,
nor with a warning, nor even the small sense
that history makes when it claims inevitability,
the torpid and horrible tide spreads over the land.
For Simon's long plans have come to fruit:
at their abject entreaties the Prophet returned to his followers,
clothed himself and issued forth from the mountain;
burned, in a black and brilliant auto-da-fé
with masks out of charivari, the bodies of those
who opposed him politically, whispering doubts of his truth.
And now he has set the faith of the counties against
the brutal oblivion of the Riots, and this time
the note is struck, and the marriage consummated.
The Burbs, cowed, are forced to withhold the Rioters' drug;
and a Jesus put in its place, whose one face
is a cookie-jar sweetness, a love that smears everyone
indiscriminately, giving to lives without meaning,
trapped in a radical furrowlessness, a warm
sun and a center; for even the way of the Riot
has not completely quenched the thirst for ideology
that raises our poor species to the light but damns it
to monstrous cruelty too; and so the other
face of the Jesus they give to the Riots is twisted
with white cold and hatred bitter as cancer
to call out a fear and obedience that will pass for a soul.
And out from the ancient cities of the Uess: Delphia,

Cargo, Baltimo, Pitsburg, Kelan, Cumbus,
and Tedo, there pours a formless mob, shepherded
here and there by appalled Black County riders,
bent, as far as their twenty-word lexicon stretches,
on crusade for the Lord and fire for the infidel damned.
They do not mark off their Messiah from the god he serves
but worship him crudely, with tears, howls, adorations.
He will lead his people into the Promised Land,
and feed his flock on the honey and milk of Paradise.

◆

Over the fields and meadows, trampling the Queen Anne's
lace and milkweed of fall they come; nothing
can stop them, they swarm in their millions like spores of a slime
mold or an infestation of naked caterpillars;
the armies of Tuscarawas, Sandusky, Wyandot
inflict great slaughter but are brushed aside;
it is as it was in the great pogrom against
the middle class of the twenty-first century. James
musters his forces and strikes their shambling columns,
but on they come, for with the unimagining
of death that the Rioters share with the beasts, they now
are promised a heaven of tasty sweetness with God.
Behind ride disciplined formations of cavalry
bearing once more the dark standards of the Raven.
As winter tightens its grip, the Free Countians
abandon their cities and flee to the hills and forests;
James takes command of the last Free forces
and covers the long retreat of civilians and government.
Ruth and many Mohicans take refuge in the woods
about the headwaters of the Mohican; other go south
and dwell in the Hocking Hills. I, your poet,
suffered from cold and hunger and lived in a cave,
and sang my songs round the fire to distract the minds
of those that I serve from the pain of their great losses;
we devised cunning games, to be played with berries
too sour to eat, and twigs, and maps marked
in the dust: we named one of them "Sperimenh's Game"
and play it now in Lent to remember the time.
That winter was evil and cold; and the next

was worse. We built in the woods shelters of logs
and fed on looted grain, wild beasts,
roots and berries in fall, May apples in spring,
dug up the bulbs of the flowers and devoured them; captured
jays and robins and cooked them whole over twigs.
The warriors aged and grew lean, and their eyes and hands
told of the horrors their lips would not tell; for the Riots
fared worse than we. James rode
with the partisans and saw a female giving birth in the snow
and a circle of Riot boys cooking what could not
be other than a human hand; a blinded horse
striking at wolves; barns of the rotting corn;
ordure on soaked carpets; Black Countian
officers smoking cigars over deep snifters
of fine Mohican brandy; a raped woman
torn to the gills; a whole tribe of Rioters
feasting on the flesh of a captured Free warrior;
fields of wheat unharvested, going to weeds.
For the most part James did not attack the Rioters,
unless they resisted him; he pitied them, the empty and desecrate
temples of the human spirit. He sought the bivouacs
of Black Countian troops, and struck without warning
from snow-muffled forests or across, at a gallop, the wastes
of the icy fields; he fired their barracks, slew
the smoke-choked survivors who stumbled out;
his rage grew hotter as winter drew on; men
and women who'd lost their farms flocked to his standard;
and always Antony rode at his right hand.

◆

In the first winter James and Ruth lost Adam
their son. He sickened with cold and hunger, shivered
and burned with the fever; his fat limbs wasted,
he forgot the words he had learned, and could not be comforted
any more by his mother; he arched his back and at last
was still, like a grey doll of a person in his little
clothes. James grew grey like the dead, and his fury
mounted and cankered within him: he wore a mask
in his raids lest folk should perceive his weeping, but said
that he wished not to be recognized; they called him "Robin"

or sometimes "Cock Robin," the fierce Free guerrillas;
and themselves were known as "Robin's Wolves." Daniel
Quincy, who'd loved his baby brother,
begged to ride with the Wolves; he was twelve but a crack
shot, and his father allowed him to come; better
corrupted by known violence than by the unknown.
Ruth grieved over her baby and felt the ice
of duty creep over her soul; many
Mohicans had lost dear kin and friends
and she, concealing the empty ache, gave them comfort;
she broke the black market, created commissions
to share the food and grow or steal what they could;
she even persuaded the strange lords of Mars
to send, on credit, a shipful of pinkish grain;
her spies told her that some Free Counties
in the west and south had survived; she salvaged a weapons shop
and dug out a cave for a microprocessor factory;
with the help of Mary Quincy the mother of James
staffed a mobile hospital and served in its wards,
while Maia, her baby, slept on her back in a sling.

♦

And sometimes, those two terrible years, they found
moments of sweetness yet in the wreck of the world.
Spring came lovely that first year;
at Easter they danced the birth of the Buddha, the Resurrection
of Christ, ate the flat bread of the Passover;
meltwater streams roared and glittered; wood
pigeons cooed sweetly in the copses; Maia,
the baby girl, blossomed and talked early;
hot nights filled with the smell of blossoms;
the column of partisans sang as they rode to battle;
Judd and Antony even got up a football game;
sick men healed, and James captured
a great train of food wagons bound for the army
of the Jihad, and they ate till they burst, and slept, and swam
in the cold streams, and ate, and sang, and gave thanks.
But all was without hope, a temporary carnival;
their arrows, guided by intelligent bows, might fly
like hail on the Black County platoons, and flames

162

might redden the snows at evening, but force would no longer
serve the enemies of the Messiah. Early next winter
James struck from the north and south at Mount Verdant,
timing the attacks superbly, covering them with a blow
against Black County positions about Mansfield and Lexington.
For nine days they held the capital, and cleared it
of enemy troops and Rioters, whom they showed to the limits.
But waves of Rioter slave troops, shoddily armed
but yelling, threw the Free forces back.
On the last day James rode through the city,
the tears pouring from under his mask: Mount Verdant
was defiled and filthy, the great dome of the Cathedral
broken, a smell of urine in its naves and apses;
the noble houses on Gambier Street were looted;
wisps of smoke rose from the blackened beams;
the Gay Street theaters had been used as brothels
where Rioter females could earn a little joyjuice
from the bored soldiers of the Jihad. Another raid
struck at three ideological retraining centers
where Black Countian dissidents were held, and freed
the living skeletons within. It was this raid
that decided Simon to play his most terrible card.

◆

At Christmas, then, his generals threw their full strength
against the woodland strongholds of the Free Counties.
It was time, the Messiah said, to pinch out
this wasp that turned them aside from the great crusade:
the whole continent lay before them, to be converted
to the Lord; it was a sin to allow those ragged brigades
to halt the holy work of Almighty God.
But James and Antony had long expected this move,
anticipated their enemies' tactics, worked out
the details in war games among the Free commanders;
the secret Mohican fiction of the Jihad's expected
campaign orders was almost word for word
the same as the reality within the dispatch case
stamped with the Raven, which the Black generals carried.
Three columns drove for the heart of the woods;
in a series of brilliant ambushes, feints, retreats,

countermarches, and lightning attacks from the trees,
the Free forces turned the advance of the enemy,
leading each column into the ravine of the Mohican;
there, in a bloody confusion, the hosts of the Jihad
slaughtered each other in blind rocket barrages
under the snow-burdened pines and spruce of the valley.
Their retreat turned into a rout, and the white-clad
partisan forces rejoined at their camp singing
about the red bonfire, with beakers of hot
spiced wine. But the great attack was only
a ruse to distract the Free commander's attention;
in the confusion Daniel Quincy has vanished
and with him Judd, the boy's quiet guardian.
Simon has called at last on the man's promise
of fealty in exchange for revenge; the boy is now
in the hands of the Black Crusade. At first the loss
is not noticed; but casual questions turn to demands
and entreaties: at last grief breaks out
in its full flood, and Ruth and James see
in each other's eyes the final wreck of their lives.

2. The Third Meeting with Kingfish

No search or inquiry reveals the boy,
and at last James comes to Catherine the seer, asks her
if Daniel is still alive and where he lies.
She dwells in a smoky wigwam roofed with bark
and stirs a pot over a glowing fire.
Swiftly her trance begins, gives way to utterance:
"He is alive; you are betrayed; Simon
his uncle holds your son; the boy does not weep
but his heart yearns for the sight of his father and mother."
Two weeks later (Simon believes
in giving to grief and uncertainty all the time
that they need to grow and luxuriate) Catherine's words
are confirmed: a message arrives by an embassy blindfolded
by Free partisans, reading as follows: "To Ruth

164

Praetor, and James, commander of rebel forces:
Congratulations on a well-fought victory.
Your son enjoys our hospitality. But we,
much though we value the young man's company,
would still prefer his father's presence instead."
The terms of the exchange, and date, follow at once:
James must pledge his honor not to attempt
by force of arms to break the contract; Ruth
must be there; Simon will meet them with thirty men
a month hence at Lithend Farm, hand over
the boy, and carry James back as a prisoner.

♦

Without James, resistance will flicker and die.
He must betray his whole people, or his son.
Husband and wife cannot bear to look at each other,
for the child they have made is now the grief of their lover.
But in despair, his mother Mary comes to him,
speaking no words, but taking his head in her arms;
and warmed a little, James goes again to Catherine,
asks her in mere humility what he can do.
She answers, saying that he must seek out once more
the old man who gave him his father's sword;
"And do not forget, this time, to ask him the question."
James sends a message to Maury Edsel, who now
has combined his enterprise with that of Douglas McCloud;
they've withdrawn their business outside the bounds of the Jihad,
have been sending, in secret, supplies to the Free forces.
An airstrip is cleared and a sunplane bumps down; over
the white and smoke-blue world, so pure
on this winter morning, James and the pilot sit
like gods, withdrawn from suffering. Extending its floats,
the craft sets down in the Hudson and James, clad
in full armor, takes the ancient path through the labyrinth,
finds at last the dim chambers where Kingfish
toils at his long tasks. This time
the old man seems to him small and gaunt
and tired, and James, despite his grief, pities him:
all through the journey James had sought in his mind
what was the question that he must ask the old man;

but now he forgets his calculations, and speaks:
"Kingfish, why do you always cry out with pain?
What wound do you carry that never abates?"

♦

"Son," says Kingfish, "now yo' done ask de question.
Thou lettest therefore the old man depart
in peace, the servant of thy people. Dat wound
was give me by mah twin brother. Ah
was de las' elected Presiden ob de United States.
But ah nevah take office; maybe ah save de Union
if ah's given a year. Mah brother Dan Petro
he a hoodoo man, he jealous ob mah election, he lay
dis curse on me, and send an arrow in de ass of de image
he make wid wax and de clippins of mah hair and nails.
When ah sick, he become Presiden, take
de oath, an' in two year enemies kill him.
Me, ah learn to bear de cancer; but de curse
be dat ah live for ever wid de pain, unless
a king come and ask me de question you ask.
Now, boy, dis ol' man can die
in peace; ah thank you, boy." "Kingfish, wait.
Do not die yet. Two gifts you gave me,
a sword and an eye. Give me one more:
my son, who lies in utter bondage to my enemy."
"Dat be one gift dis ol' man
caint give you, son. Be brave. We all
alone here in dis world. Ah give you one
mo' gift, but ah ain't got no power
any more to give it: permission." "Permission for what?"
"Permission to break yo' own honor, man. Dat's
de gift. If yo' think it ain't such a gift yo' don'
got no need to take it. Ah so tired.
De pain done all gone away. Go, Robin de King;
yo' got possession now. Yo' honor is yours;
yo' spend it however yo' like. Goodbye." As if
he bent to see something closely held in his hands
Kingfish leans forward in his throne, and dies;
a small dwarf in blue overalls, quite
still, hunched over on a chair in the dark.

166

◆

As the sunplane banks and drones through the skies of Vaniah
James remembers moment by moment his life,
striving to see the sense of it all, Kingfish
dead, and his last gift, that vile permission,
hanging upon him like the taste of a nightmare: the days
as a child at Lithend, his playfellows Ruth, Simon,
and Antony; his father's disgrace, the exile in Hattan;
the fight with the Slob and the first encounter with Kingfish;
the battles at Triadelphia and St. Clair, the return to Mohican;
the lovely intelligence of Ruth, the conversation
under the ginkgos, the three tests of the suitors;
the greatness and death of Shaker McCloud, the grief
of Ruth's coldness, the wars with Simon's crusade,
the second meeting with Kingfish, the strange adventures
in lake and sky, the great blessing of return,
teaching Daniel his books, riding, the way
of the plow, McArgus trotting along behind;
those sweet years when they swore that no grief,
succeeding, might wipe away the glory and the joy
of perfect love; the garden by the river, run
now to seed or dead with the frost. As he flies
westward, it becomes clear to him that he must say
goodbye to his life, and it grieves him, for he has loved
his life; and that he must also bid farewell
to Ruth, his lover and friend and warm wife;
he draws Adamant from its scabbard, and looks upon it;
his head nods, and exhausted, he falls asleep
for the first time in many days; he dreams
of the time, late last summer when the war
had abated and Adam's death was briefly forgotten,
how he and Ruth had taken a basket of bread
and cheeses and fruit, and wandered together down
by the bright waters of the Mohican; how in the meadow
they'd stripped and lay in the sun; her body white
but flowered with a foam of freckles, set with crimson
and coral, hazed with a fiery halo of hair;
how age had only deepened the forms of her cheekbone
and chin, and left a long lovely line

167

from eye to corner of mouth; how their kisses seemed,
like sweet cold water after long toil,
never to lose their freshness, and how, that moment
her dark brown eyes opened suddenly
and she laughed in her nest of green and golden grass.

♦

When he wakes they are bouncing over the field to a stop.
He finds that his dream has caused him to seize his sword
and grip it tightly, and despite the care of its mind,
the blade has slightly cut the flesh of his palm.
As he stumbles out of the plane, he shakes the blood
from his hand, which leaves a heavy blot in the snow
of crimson, and a trail of sallower coral; the blue
twilight is almost come, and the colors blaze
in the dead of winter. James gasps, and tears
burst from his eyelids: for the colors remind him of Ruth
in her nakedness lying asleep; and the pilot shakes him
and cannot break his paralysis, standing stupidly
staring down at the snow. It is only when he,
the pilot, has obscured the drops of blood with his body
that James is able to draw his eyes away
and plod forward to join his desolate people.

3. The Fall of the King

James sends to Simon that he accepts the terms;
and so, on an evening heavy with threat of snow,
four cloaked and hooded shapes ride
from the camp: three queens with pale faces
and a haggard king riding a silver mare
whose sire was Gringolet. Ruth is there, and Mary,
the boy's grandmother, and Catherine the seer whose request
to come with them James has strangely granted, in return
for a certain service he has asked her to render to him.
As Simon demands, James is unarmed; only
a brooch of gold in the form of a ginkgo leaf

glows at his shoulder as a sign to the Messiah's guards.
Their road takes them through Avalon Valley; the orchards
are bare, the apple groves blossom only with snow.
As they pass the gingerbread house of Faith Raven
the old woman comes out to watch them go by:
though she's old, she's hale, and it seems she will live for ever.
They do not speak to her, nor does she break the silence,
but they feel her eyes on their backs far down the way.

♦

The great hall of Lithend Farm is draped
in black, to honor the presence of the Messiah. James
is searched, but Simon rests secure in his word
of honor not to attempt a better bargain
by force of arms, and the three ladies are scarcely
given a glance: the guards cannot bear Catherine's
frightening eyes. A throne has been set on a dais
where once James carved for his friends and family,
and children laughed to see him pretend to be fierce.
Simon broods on the high seat, his plans
almost perfectly come to fruition, his eyes
black as the ravens embroidered into the black
silk of his standard. Before him on either side
stand at attention nine armed men,
the pick of his guard. Behind him the Twelve Elders,
his chief advisors; there is no sign of the boy.

♦

"Welcome," says Simon, "to the house of our father in heaven.
We shall live together at home, as is right for brothers;
of course, my lady," he bows to Ruth, "if you wish
to join your family we shall be truly delighted.
It is so hard to part with your well-behaved son."
Ruth shudders, but does not speak; the red
spots on his cheeks suddenly darken. But he turns
to Mary and Catherine. "What an honor, ladies,
to receive you here. May I call you mother, since,
truly, you are the wife of my father? And you,
sister; I did not expect the pleasure of your company,
but perhaps you wished to see your brother again."

They do not reply, but James looks at the ceiling.
"Where is my son?" he demands after a silence.
"Ah," says Simon; "I had forgotten." He claps,
and a door opens: Daniel appears, pale,
with Judd behind him. James glances at the traitor
who will not meet his eyes. Very quietly, James
speaks to the boy. "Are you all right, my love?"
he asks; and Daniel nods. "Hand him over,"
he says, "let us waste no time." Judd releases him;
Daniel walks, controlled, across to his mother.
As he does so James steps forward, caresses
the head of the boy as he passes, and turns when he reaches
the ranks of the Raven Guard. He unpins his cloak,
letting it fall, and holds up the golden brooch,
the ginkgo leaf of his personal crest. "And thus,"
says James, "I break my honor. Let no one speak
to me more." He bends the beautiful gold till it snaps,
and dashes the fragments to the floor. It is a signal;
Catherine reaches into her cloak and withdraws
the sword Adamant, and tosses it over to James.
It spins, turns, and he catches it by the hilt. The guards,
stunned, begin to draw their weapons; but James
leaps to the wall and with one stroke strikes
through the hangings of black, through fine wood paneling,
down to the great cable that carries the power
of the house and farm; knowing its path as a man
knows the veins in his own wrist, James
has severed the superconductor cleanly; a burst of sparks,
and the lights go out, leaving the hall in darkness.
But for James there is no darkness; his marvelous eye
discerns the ghostly bodies of men, and the odds
are evened as he dresses him once again to battle.
The slaughter is terrible; eighteen men in full armor
stand between James and the man he seeks to destroy,
and bestial shrieks follow the path of the sword;
James is wounded twice, but cuts his way
to the throne. Adamant burns in his hand; the surge
of current has burst the sword's capacitors; only
emergency circuitry slows the death of the weapon
and gives to its master a last access of power.

And now with a boom, a blaze ignites where the sparks
from the severed cable have caught on the torn silk
of the hangings. The room, with its carnage, is lit brightly:
at the end of the hall Daniel and Ruth have armed
themselves with a sword and a halberd gleaned from the dead;
between James and his loved ones a waste of wounded and dying;
behind, twelve cowering counselors, and there
before him, Simon, standing calmly, his sword
drawn and a smile on his hurt and bitter lips.
"Who wounds my flesh," he says, "is cursed, for upon his head
lies the death of all my true disciples. My blood
defiles my murderer and carries him down into Hell."
"What do I care?" says James; "for I am a man
who has lost his honor, and every curse you can utter
slakes the thirst for pain that masters my life.
Come on." They meet, strike, parry, as flames
ripple and roar on the wall. But the rage of James
George Quincy, Rollo the swordfinder, Jago
the scourge of the dark crusade, Robin the eater
of raw flesh, the wolf of the great snow,
cannot be balked. For evil is capable only
of evil; but good, being master of good, is master
also of evil, and roused to evil is powerful
far beyond the dreams of the evil. Do not
untie the knot of the good; for order and form,
like matter, are woven of energy bound to itself
so tight that the swiftness of knowledge, of light, must be bred
with itself to describe the fury pent in the grain.
And now the paneling burns, and the heat reddens
the faces of both of the brothers; Simon hews
at the waist of his enemy; James leaps in the air
and the blow passes beneath; Adamant whines
and through armor, flesh, and bone, the sword
of his father sinks to rest in the Messiah's side.
Simon's weapon drops from his hand, and he stoops;
James raises his sword. But at that moment
one of the strewn bodies moves in the hall.
It is Judd, stunned by a blow but groping for his knife;
he rises up on his knees and plunges the blade
deep in the back of his master James. The hero

171

feels the grate of steel on his backbone; and suddenly
Adamant, seeking to spill the energy stored
in its circuitry, glows white hot at the tip;
the heat cannot swiftly enough be lost to the air
and a great fat drop of molten steel
trembles and falls: the sword is beginning to melt.
The sword's master melts too; his knees
buckle, and he falls down before his enemy.
Simon, holding his side, prepares to make
for the door, and safety; but cannot resist the contempt
and rage he feels for his servant Judd, who has saved
his life but has never known the dark truth
that Simon has served all these years. "Fool!" says Simon;
"It was I that slew your brother, not the man
you have stabbed in the back. He was your kind friend.
Why will they never learn?" He turns, but the moment's
delay is enough. Three queens in the firelight,
eyes glittering in their pale faces, Ruth,
Mary, and Catherine, rise up around him like shadows.
Their long knives, the knives of Kshatriya ladies,
rise up, and fall; he shrieks, and tries to escape;
the blades, running with black blood, rise
again and bury themselves in the flesh of that man
whose life, so unhappy, has fled from its torment at last.

◆

But Daniel kneels over his father, the tips
of his golden hair beginning to flare into flame
with the heat of the fire; he is weeping. The three women
lift the body and bear it towards the door.
But one more terrible deed must be acted
here in the house of flame. Judd, who was silent,
hearing his life deceived and his faith turned to treachery
finds at last the strength of utterance. No
words, but an unforgettable cry; he raises
his knife, and sinks it deep in his own heart;
the blood boils by the hilts. At this, the chief
counselor rouses himself; he has not understood,
nor have his peers, the apocalypse they have just witnessed,
but seeing his master, the only Messiah, dead

172

at the hands of witches, and this one man
his servant, whose will is, as it seems, hardy
enough to follow; the counselor feels himself shamed
and upbraided to do the like. In a moment he falls,
his knife in his ribs. Another counsellor raises
a dagger, but now a third holds his hand back.
"Wait! Time enough when the Faithful are told
and shown the path of their duty. You heard His words:
that the True Disciples must die if the Master's flesh
is breached and desecrated. Let us go where He has gone,
follow Him into the better world of the ever-
living; but His flock must not be left behind
in the world dark by His passing. Courage, friends;
we come to our Master when all His bidding is done."
A beam, crackling with flames, falls from the ceiling;
now all the living break for the doors and stumble
out into snow lit by the winter moon.

◆

As the three queens, grieving, ride back with the wreck
of their hero and the chilled grief of his son, they pass
once more through the valley of apples; there, by the house,
a dark smudge like a huge dead bird
lies in the snow. It is Faith, who has known by her arts
the spirit's passing of her son, and whose heart, poisoned
by hatred and grief, has broken and cast her down
as she stared at the great halo of red on the skyline
where Lithend burned as once it burned when Shaker
McCloud her enemy lay in his blood on the Hill.
They pass her by, but folk came later
and buried her as she set it down in her will,
not prone but standing, beneath the thresholds of Avalon;
Those who lived there afterwards suffered bad luck
and sickness, and an old woman walked by night
and a raven perched on the roof-tree by day. At last
the place was deserted; other men came and dug up
the bones, and buried them further away, stretched out
on their back, as is custom. And after that the place
was quiet and all ill happenings ceased.

4. Sacrifice

At midnight the riders come to the camp of the partisans.
They find Antony waiting beside a great fire:
he had wished to be with them, but James had dissuaded him, citing
the need for a Free general should James be lost,
and the likely suspicions of Simon should Antony come.
As they enter the firelight Antony blows a great horn
and folk come forth to carry the hero James
to the crude field hospital under the trees.
Ruth, the leader of her people, speaks to the host
that assembles about the fire. "First, friends,
we have great cause for rejoicing. Our enemy, Simon,
is dead, and the fire has eaten his bones. Without him,
his armies and slaves are like ice that melts in the spring.
And I, a mother, am more lucky than many
who have lost not one child but all; my son
is restored to me. But greater than these happy events
is the grief that has come on us all, and on me in especial;
James George Quincy is wounded grievously,
perhaps unto death; he got his wound fighting
for you, and for me and my son. Forgive me, friends,
if I leave you now to attend my husband; your homes
and your lands have been bought back for you by his pains."

◆

And Daniel, the son of James, shows to the people
the tall scabbard he has carried back from the fire:
he draws the sword that it holds, but to the terror and sorrow
of all that look on, the blade is only a stump
melted and fused, the lovely riverlike blue
of the steel blackened and rainbowed with the rot of its crystals;
Adamant, the sword of George Quincy, that Kingfish
saved from the Riots and gave to his son James,
has died in its master's service, and burning to death
has taken good care not to singe or scorch his hand.
The sword is laid on the bed of the hero in honor.
Around him the doctors have worked, and made their diagnosis:
the man that they tend is broken by fever and weariness,

having for months denied himself food and sleep;
he is weak with loss of blood from the two wounds
dealt him by Simon's guard; but worst of all,
the blow of the traitor Judd has severed his spine
and the fine hierarchy that binds the brain to the limbs
is broken, the chain of mastering life is shattered,
and the legs and trunk, naked now to the healers,
so wasted and aged untimely and yet so beautiful,
lie like the dumb earth of the field, flesh
without sense, as if the choice of the Riots to forget
their humanity fell on the limbs of their mightiest scourge.

◆

In the morning an odd silence hangs over the land.
The scouts report no enemy activity;
a patrol pushes out to the small town of Loudonville
on the edge of the forest, and finds the place quiet and still;
there is no response when they probe the outskirts, and none
when they seize the public square. One of the soldiers
hears a baby cry in a rubbish heap;
removing the filth they find a cradle and in it
a child. A young Mohican woman, a corporal,
breaks open the door of the town meeting hall
used, as is frequent, as a church by the Messiah's worshipers.
The door opens with difficulty: a corpse
has jammed it. Within, a heap of dead can be seen,
and beyond, up the stairs to the main hall, windrows
of corpses, no apparent wound, and the hall,
beyond, is heaped with slaughter: they have stood packed,
and when they fell they twisted this way and that
as ripe wheat will when lodged by a storm,
or forests tumbled and swept by the black tornado.
Two of the younger boys, recent recruits,
are sick, and must be relieved. Another is sent
to carry the news to the camp of the partisans.

◆

It was the self-slaying of Judd the traitor that began it:
The Messiah's faithful apostles carried the word
to the hosts that served him, and called them to follow their master;

the Black County warriors, obeying not only the code
of the vengeful Lord, but also their Kshatriya honor,
have spread the message of death, and most, the courageous,
have wreaked on themselves the letter of the Elders' commands.
The weaker, in terror and shame, or even relief,
have saddled their horses and ride for their farms and homes.
The Word of Death has fallen on fertile ground:
both Mad Countians and Rioters have suffered greatly
from hunger, disease, cold, and the breaking of customs,
the raids of the Free partisans, the scorched earth
of war, the deprivation of known comforts,
the vicious and frightening luxuries of the victor, or the loss,
for the Riots, of their joyjuice supply; and the fear of the Lord,
and the fear of those whose land and homes they have spoiled.
That voluptuous panic and sweet paranoia
that carry a mind to self-extinction, has risen
like yeasty foam to the surface, and burst; the call
of the mass, the homely feeling of family among all
the people one knows, has made it terribly hard
to stay behind. Great vats of joyjuice
poisoned with strychnine have been swiftly prepared by the Elders;
the people herded, with prayer and song, to the halls;
the death sacrament passed from hand to hand,
mothers helping their babies to suck down the sweetness,
brave little boys carrying jugs of the elixir
here and there; the prayers turning to screams
of abandon, mystic rapture, terror, despair.
All over Ahiah the millions have perished,
and lie like a blight on the cities and villages; silence
and dawn; the calling of a few winter birds.

♦

What are the thoughts of those Free citizens, given
once more their homes and their lands, at such fearful cost?
Some of the first to go back are ridden by nightmares and fall
into sleepless insanity. Ruth seeks to keep
her people back in the clean forests, till strong-
hearted soldiers have cleared the towns and cities of dead;
great pits are dug, and the frozen bodies
are tumbled in, and covered with lime, and buried;

176

but a thaw sets in before the work is completed
and soon the streets are sweet and heavy with the stench
of death, and nowhere is free of it; disease breaks out
in several places, for many have disobeyed
the command to remain in the camps. At first the Free
folk, as is natural, fall into great rejoicing;
but as the scope of the hand of death is revealed
and the numbers of dead seem infinite, as if all of history's
crimes had buried their foulness here in this century,
and now the victims had worked their way to the surface
to accuse the living: so a cloud comes over the Free
that turns to a black haze of flies and death
in the premature spring that follows that terrible winter.
And even after the last of the rotting dead
heavy with juice and boiling with green corruptions
has been covered over with neutral and innocent soil
the great shadow of guilt hangs over the land
of Mohican, and the green spring's infancy is spoiled.
Worst of all, the people withdraw to themselves,
and lose that humane and civic nobility which stamps
the Free person with higher concerns than his own.
That withdrawal created, back in the twentieth
century, the first seeds of the Riots themselves:
it seems that the death of the Riots will spawn them anew.
The public discourse is tainted, like water that holds
however faint and dilute, the taste of foulness;
and as a sign, a beastly crime is committed:
the rape and murder of a girl in dear old Mansfield,
the first such crime by Mohicans in ten years.
Meanwhile James is moved to Mount Verdant Hospital
but continues to burn with fever and waste away;
and still he wanders the dull caves of delirium
where words take on an unnatural force and density
like the poems they wrote in the early years of the Great
Pogrom; and a ball of hair and sickening satin
pursues him down the labyrinths of his evil dreams.

◆

And Ruth must carry the burden of both sicknesses:
cheerful always in public, and very efficient,

she mobilizes all the ordered resources
of rational thought and the Mohican constitution:
and Antony stands at her right hand, the power
and strength to execute what she commands. But nought
will avail; and at last she turns to her sister Catherine.
"Cathy," she says, "we shall lose the life of our county
if no cure can be found for the pollution she suffers.
I carry James' baby in my womb, but I fear
she will never be born if the curse cannot be removed.
What must be done to cleanse my people of guilt?"
And from her trance Catherine sighs, and speaks.
"The god Sperimenh is sick, and the god Pan
is angry. Pray to Yahman, the purifier; let
there be a day of worship, and then to you
will appear a fitting sacrifice, an acceptable offering
that Pan be appeased and Sperimenh healed of her sickness."

◆

And so the old cathedral is swept and washed
of the filth left by the Rioters; the broken dome
is patched, till a new one be blown; the monk Robert
is called on to lead the Free people in prayer.
And one day James wakes in the hospital
not clouded by madness, nor pain, but in fear
of the dream he has dreamed: that Ruth stands at the altar,
a knife in her hand, and weeps and weeps without ceasing:
and there on the stone before her lies their son
Daniel, whom she must slay in her office of priestess.
A strange silence hangs over the city, but he sees
through the window the sun shine on the treetops, and hears
a sweet bird sing. An immense boom
beats in the air: the great glass bell
in the tower has tolled, and strikes again and again:
it is Easter day and the bell calls him to church.
But he knows quite clearly that he is dying; and his feet
will not obey him, and his strength is faint and distant.
The stump of his sword lies on the coverlet: seizing it
he feels a strange power come into his arms.
He jerks the white tubes and filaments from his body

and calls for his nurse and commands him to bring his clothes;
and such is the force and authority of his eyes and voice
that the man obeys, and assists him to dress. Now
he orders the man to lift him, and carry him down
to the church; but the man is reluctant, till James begins
to drag himself over the floor. White-faced,
the man lifts his master up on his back
and carries him out in the air. A few stragglers,
hurrying not to miss the last stroke
of the bell, see them there, and bear the news
to the worshipers: Siddhartha, Robert, the brother of Ruth,
has just begun the ritual sacrifice, hopeless
and strange, for at the demand of Ruth, no
victim, ram or heifer or lamb, is prepared,
and they stand empty-handed, Ruth, Robert, and Daniel
about the bare black altar of Yahman;
only Ruth's knife, the bane of Simon
the dark Messiah, lies on the naked stone.

♦

At the porch of Yahman James demands of the man
who bears him, that he be put down. For the last scene
he must act and suffer alone, lest his deeds contaminate
others; he crawls to the altar, and past it, sinking
the stump of the sword in the floor to drag him along.
The people in terror draw aside, and Ruth,
even, is warned by a look to leave him alone.
At the central hub or crotch of the church he stops
and gasps. There is no altar under the broken
dome at the center; the clay figure that hung
from the eye of the rose has been smashed by the Black Crusade.
James chooses one of the six compound
piers that support the dome, between the naves
of Pan and Sperimenh, but closer to Sperimenh, facing
across the pit and down the nave of Yahman.
And now with his hands and sword he draws himself up
as a boy will climb up the trunk of a tree to attain
the first branch, and pull himself over; with the effort
one of the wounds on his breast bursts open

179

and blood stains the beautiful cloth of his cloak.
He has wedged the sword between two delicate columns
that cluster and twine and fuse like roots, to support him;
and now with one hand he unbuckles the belt
of fine leather and gold that Shaker gave him;
the tongue in his teeth, he binds the belt around one
of the pillars, and about his breast, and buckles it there.
The people have come up around and watch in silence:
from Ruth's eyes tears pour down
for she knows now what James must do and cannot
prevent him. When his breathing subsides he begins to speak.
"Do not pity me, friends, for I of all men
have been most happy, and happiness need not be carried
down to the grave, but remains in the light of the world.
But the tree of my spine is shattered, my honor is broken,
I have done what I came into the world to do,
and I leave my people in the hands of one that I trust,
my sweet love in the hands of my friend and comrade,
my son with the memory of one, not at the end
the model of promises kept, but a loving father;
and to my great joy, beyond all grief of farewell,
I see now that I leave my wife with child;
therefore I part from my dear life willingly
and give to you, as a cup of wine is passed
from one to another, that sweetness I borrowed in my time.
And I know the defilement and cloud that has fallen upon you,
and I know that you lack a proper and acceptable sacrifice;
and so I give you this body, broken as it is,
and smudged with dishonor, to carry all of your guilt
down with it into the ground; where,
my good friends, like the foulness of animals spread
on the fields and turned under the soil, it may nourish
all of the lovely gardens of our dear land.
Do not weep. I am no more than the golden leaf
that falls from the tree. Mother, it hurts. Be over
soon. Goodbye." And now the hero sighs,
and hauls himself up with his arms, and sighs again,
and the light fades, for a cloud passes over the dome;
and he sighs again, and his head drops, and a crack
runs up the tall pillar that holds him upright,

and his spirit, completed, begins its journey to the world.
And it seems to all present that the dome and the apse
of Pan glow with enormous light, that spreads
to the naves of Yahman and Sperimenh; the spring cloud
with blinding skirts has passed from the face of the sun.
And each person seems to taste that food
which is most delicious to him; and a scent of spring,
of blossoms of apples, or wind on a hilltop, or daffodils,
blows through and fills the tall spaces of the cathedral;
and strangest of all, though every person grieves
with full measure according to the height of his loss,
yet a joy also brims up in him, a lightness
from any cares in the world, like lying awake
in the first morning of a holiday, hearing the breakfast
dishes being set out, and birds by the window,
and fresh suds in a tub that rasp in the sun.
And from that moment the curse of the Free Counties
is removed; and though memory and careful historians
wisely and soberly still recall for the future
the terrible days of the past, yet the evil remains
with the dead, and does not any longer stick to the living.

◆

There before them, as they leave the church doors,
is a world free of the stain of the past. Ruth
will mourn, but as James has bidden, will marry at last
her old friend and lover Antony, and so
he will be blessed for his long patience and loyalty.
And presently over the stone drum of the church
will hang a beautiful new-blown dome
dangling in the blue from a giant crimson and yellow
dirigible sent by the firm of Edsel-McCloud,
the workmen carefully guiding the rim to its rest;
and the baby girl will be born, and named Perdita,
and she will be wise like Catherine in the ways of the spirit;
and Ruth and Antony will find that the garden at Lithend
in the vale of Les Tres Riches Heures is little damaged
and within a year will bloom as richly as ever;
and the farm at Lithend rebuilt, and the wheat whitening.
Hand in hand Ruth and her son Daniel

stand for a moment there on the steps of the church
together, as once James Quincy the hero
and Mary his mother stood on a Vanian hill
and breathed the wind that blows from the edge of time,
and looked on the far fields of their native land.

PRINCETON SERIES OF CONTEMPORARY POETS

◆

LIBRARY OF CONGRESS CATALOGING IN PUBLICATION DATA

◆

Turner, Frederick, 1943-
The new world.

(Princeton series of contemporary poets)
I. Title. II. Series.
PS3570.U69N48 1985   811'.54   84-24788
ISBN 0-691-06641-8   ISBN 0-691-01420-5 (pbk.)